A SPEAKER'S GUIDE TO
EFFECTIVE
COMMUNICATION

Geoffrey Smith

"You alone are limited nowhere. You can choose to be whatever you decide to be according to your own will. Not heavenly, not mortal, not immortal, did I create you. For you yourself shall be your own master and builder and creator according to your own will and your own honour. So, you are free to sink to the lowest level of the animal kingdom but you may also soar into the highest spheres of creation."

Pico Della Mirandola (1463 – 1494)
Italian Renaissance Philosopher.
Oration on the Dignity of Man

ISBN: 978-0-9738509-1-8

I dedicate this book to my son Nicholas and his wife Nancy, to my daughter Mandy and her husband Derek, to my wife Miriam, my beloved grandchildren Sebastian, Bianca, Angelica, Victoria, Myles, Jayden and Alessia and to all those other generations waiting patiently in the wings for their entrance into this beautiful experience we call life. Thank you for giving so much meaning to mine.

Additionally, to Kendall. A beautiful golden retriever who for 12 wonderful years taught me the importance of the present moment, of unconditional love and an acceptance of that which we cannot change.

Finally, to that incredible organisation "Toastmasters International" and its dedicated members who, over 45 years of membership, have taught me the meaning of friendship, dedication and commitment.

To all of the above, I thank you.
Geoff Smith. DTM
Thornhill, Ontario,
Canada, June 2021.

Acknowledgments

How much we owe to the labours of others! They dig far from the sun, that we may be warm, fight in outposts of peril that we may be secure and brave unknown terrors for truths that shed light on our way"
Anonymous

In writing this book I am deeply indebted to the many wonderful people who have inspired me by their wisdom, courage and friendship. Each of them in their own way, and by advice and example, have provided the framework from which I have constructed a life of meaning, experience and inspiration. There are too many to thank specifically by name, most of you know who you are, and those who do not and who I love and admire from a distance will continue to remain unaware of my anonymous admiration and affection.

However, I will mention that wonderful leadership and public speaking organisation - Toastmasters International - for the inspiration that its wonderful and dedicated members and program have given me over 45 years of membership. It is mainly in response to that, that this book has been written.

I would like to specifically remember my mother Lilian, a wonderful woman whose calm endurance, love and warmth I cherish through the long years and to my father Clifford a kind and gentle man to whom I should have shown greater compassion and taken the time patience and understanding to know better.

Such are often the follies of youth.

Books by Geoff Smith include:

The Art of Effective Living

A Speaker's Guide to Effective Communication

The Brotherhood of Ulan and other Mystery Stories

Introduction

In their need to create a title for a book a writer seeks to achieve two goals which together reinforce each other. The first, is to capture the attention, interest and empathy of a potential reader and second, to ensure that it truly conveys the writer's intention. In this *"A Speaker's Guide to Effective Communication"* I believe that I have achieved the first.

Effective communication is a vitally important skill which enhances, progressively develops and beautifies both our human life and those upon whom it impacts, it fulfils a basic human need and can indeed be learned. I believe these certainly fulfil the first of these goals.

I have found that the second goal of using the right title to convey my intention has to be more specific in that it is initially written to inspire not only those who believe in the vital importance and power of communication as a vital survival skill, but also to those who purposely pursue it as a form of developmental practice. Most importantly, that which is expressed by the spoken word in a public context. Indeed, the history of our species shows clearly that its advancement from barbarism to civilisation and sadly on one particular occasion from civilisation to barbarism has been motivated by this form of communication which has its roots in our basic survival instinct.

This instinct is primarily filled by our ability to communicate with the world around us. Let us look more deeply into communication itself, its true meaning and driving force.

"You need other people in order to survive and your commitment to fulfilling that need is the key to your survival. Effective communication is how we do so."

Prior to writing this book I contacted many men and women who had become eminently successful in their field of endeavour. My question which was not pre-empted in any way was this: *"What single quality or factor do you think has contributed primarily to your success?"* As was to be expected high on the list was personal motivation, opportunity from birth, important social contacts, natural talent, emotional maturity and many others. However, the most important, unquestionably, were their very often inherent verbal skills backed to a great extent by body language and empathic and written ones. It is the first of these three, namely the skills of speaking, empathy and body language that are primarily discussed in this book.

Effective writing is also a vital part of communication, the importance of which is often overlooked. This includes business writing, writing for the media, literary writing, article writing and writing of a more direct and personal nature. These specifics however, although important, are beyond the scope of this book but many of the principles remain the same.

In the second paragraph of this introduction, I suggested that finding an appropriate title to convey my intention was more complex in that I wanted to convey the vital importance of communication as an inherent survival skill. This is basically discussed in the first four chapters. However, I also wanted to direct it more specifically to those who also believe in communication as a vital skill but who also practice and develop it regularly as a form of personal commitment.

It is to the latter group and very especially to that amazing, training, leadership and developmental organisation *"Toastmasters International"* of which I have been a proud member for over 45 years and its members that this book wishes to particularly honour.

However, I have to say that but for the first four chapters which outline my fervent and passionate belief in the power of communication, this book would not have been written at all. It is my sincere hope that those who believe in the former will be inspired to pursue the latter.

Geoffrey Smith. DTM.
Thornhill, Ontario, Canada.
June 2021.

Contents

Chapter 1. Major Assumptions

*What is effective communication and why do we need it...
The four essential levels of communication... The importance
of empathy.*

- Page 1 -

Chapter 2. Essential Basics of Communication

*Major communication tools... Knowing what you want to do,
communicate and achieve... Communication in leadership.*

- Page 17 -

Chapter 3. Listening

*Effective listening and its importance... Listening versus
hearing... Five steps to effective listening.*

- Page 39 -

Chapter 4. Using Communication Skills to Resolve Conflict.

*What is conflict?... Causes of conflict...Return of power...
Reinforcement of value...Resolving conflict by using your
communication skills.*

- Page 49 -

Chapter 5. Conversational Speaking

*General tips for conversational speaking...With your kids...
With your boss... With your family...With a service provider.*

- Page 63 -

Chapter 6. Effective Public Speaking.

Introduction to public speaking...Major guide lines...
Preparation...Practice...Self-confidence... Creating an
award-winning speech...Structure... Hook... Content ...
Close... Body Language... Sound... Words.

- Page 83 -

Chapter 7. Public Speaking – more specifics

The Art of Effective Debate... Persuasion techniques ...
Spontaneous speaking---Visual aids...Dealing with questions
and answers.

- Page 103 -

Chapter 8. Effective Speech Evaluation

Introduction to speech evaluation ... five approaches to
effective evaluation ... (structure ... style ... mission ...
interest ... sound)

- Page 117 -

Chapter 9. The Mysterious Art of Storytelling.

Narrative...Pauses...Surprise ... Mystery... Message
Exaggeration ... voice variation.

- Page 135 -

CHAPTER ONE
Major Assumptions of Communication

> *What is effective communication and why do we need it... The four essential levels of good communication... The importance of empathy.*

"The big problem is that most people do not listen to understand. They listen in order to reply"

Anonymous.

"To truly communicate you need to have sympathy for the aged and sick, tolerance for the misguided and weak, understanding for the young, respect for those who strive and forgiveness for those who do wrong. Each of us will face the challenge of each of these. The question is, will be worthy of that challenge?"

Geoff Smith. The Art of Effective Living.

"Always communicate in the language of the listener but think like a wise man"

William Butler Yeats.

"You need other people in order to survive and your commitment to that need is the key to your survival"

Geoff Smith. The Art of Effective Living.

Aristotle wrote, *"self – sufficiency is among the greatest of felicities."* However, to be able to enjoy, and then thrive in our own company exclusively and to fully provide for our own needs is an ideal to which many aspire but which very few ever achieve.

In reality we are all dependent upon and interdependent with, all those around us. No one can live as a hermit or monk and believe for one moment that they are *totally* independent of others. *The fact of the matter is that we need other people in order to survive effectively and our commitment to that need is the key to that survival.* This commitment is manifest and energised by our ability to communicate. This is so important that I will repeat it.

"We need other people in order to survive effectively and our commitment to that need is the key to our survival. This commitment is fulfilled, manifest and energised by our ability to communicate"

It is therefore vital that we understand and develop an effective way of relating with others in order to fill this need.

From the moment we are born and leave the unity, security and comfort of our mother's womb, it seems that we never really get over the anguish of separation and the need to overcome it. It is this feeling of separateness that is often the source of much of our anxiety and it is the need to overcome it that is our main motivator.

A baby knows instinctively, although certainly not consciously, that its survival depends on its ability to communicate. In order to be fed, comforted or released from fear it cries, looks around for a loved one and quickly learns to smile. Thus, begins its first magical journey into communication and as we grow older *the need to persuade our environment to meet our survival needs grows.* There are two paths that this may take. The mature individual, in gradually accepting the reality of separateness, quickly learns how to fuse their own reality with that of others and it is that process that I refer to as effective communication. In its finest expression this manifests as love, commitment and creativity.

Conversely, immature individuals who do not accept it, pursue the quest for unity by either becoming part of another by a needy dependence or by making others part of themselves by control.

Both these paths, namely integration or dependence/ control of others, contribute to the development of one's positive or negative self-image and self-esteem.

The first path however, in its full acceptance of the reality and separateness of others, leads to freedom, growth and enhanced survival while the latter, which denies it, leads to neurosis, and a failure to achieve any form of unity to madness.

It can be said that your relationship with others is essentially self-serving and to people brought up in the tradition that unselfish behaviour is more virtuous are completely missing the point, in that our survival *depends* on our interdependence with others, and that communication is the key to that relationship. *Authentic human development demands a realization that the apparent conflict between the needs of others and of ourselves is an illusion.*

What then is an optimum way of dealing with others? The major prerequisite is effective communication.

An essential step is to realize the similarity of our mutual needs and to use that awareness to transform those who are indifferent to you into your friends and supporters.

Before discussing the imperative need that all of us have for others, please refer once more to the statement made earlier: *"You need other people in order to survive and your commitment to fulfilling that need is the key to your survival. Effective communication is how we do so.*

Is it difficult to change and develop your communication skills and do we need to be constantly aware of the need to do so? The answer is no! as habit is the key to both. Were you aware of every stop light you approached driving to work this morning? Do you remember and practice the specific dynamics of riding a bicycle whenever you mount one? or indeed the myriad other things you do daily as a habit? It's the same with communication skills. Develop the habit of practicing them and much of your life will change and this change will then become automatic.

As mentioned above an essential step is to realize the similarity of our mutual needs and to use that awareness to transform those who are indifferent to you into your friends and supporters.

As an English social commentator once wrote:

"Our true social mission in life should be to change those who are indifferent to us into our friends and our friends into even greater ones, because the truth is that we cannot really afford one real enemy" (Lord Chesterfield in Letters to My Son).

Before discussing the imperative need that all of us have for others, please refer once more to the statement made earlier: *"You need other people in order to survive and your commitment to fulfilling that need is the key to your survival. Effective communication is how we do so."*

In their social environment, many people like to believe that they do not need others and that this is an expression of strength. Although most of us are usually prepared to admit that we enjoy others and that they contribute to our well-being, needing them is often seen as a weakness. In some ways this feeling is understandable, as the less dependent we are upon others, the less we feel at risk.

The uncomfortable truth is that we have never been totally free of the need for others and the need to communicate with them. None of us are born with all the talents needed for survival.

In primitive societies people needed others to help protect them from wild animals, to join in projects that needed varying skills, to protect their families and possessions from other groups and to merge the skills of their group with those of others to enhance their security.

In the primitive societies of Anglo-Saxon England for example, it was the gradual merging of the farming Anglos, who lacked the fighting skills to defend their farms, with the fearsome Saxon warriors, who lacked farming skills, which created the Anglo-Saxon cultural tradition. In more advanced societies like ours, those skills have become even more specialized and the need for interdependence is even greater than it has ever been.

We all need doctors to heal us, builders to house us, farmers to feed us and warriors to defend us. Within each of these groups there are many specializations. Warriors have become soldiers, policemen, firemen and ambulance drivers, farmers have become bakers, cooks and dairymen; builders have become plumbers, electricians and painters and doctors have become nurses, surgeons and social workers, each providing the multitude of skills that are counted upon for survival.

But it is not only your social needs that others fulfil. Psychologically, your growth and emerging identity are directly dependent upon feedback from the people around you, *their positive or negative reflection of your value being what ultimately develops and maintains your identity.*

It is a basic fact that our life is shaped by those who love us, and also those who refuse to love us and as John Powell the great Jesuit theologian so wisely suggested, *"Human beings, like plants, grow in the soil of acceptance, not in an atmosphere of rejection."*

Our emotional needs also demand an ever-increasing union with the world around us and the amazing thing about sharing ourselves in this manner is that it increases our joy and reduces our pain.

Erich Fromm describes this quest for union in his book, *"The Art of Loving."* He suggests that the true meaning behind the biblical symbolism of Adam and Eve has been obscured by prudery. The shame of Adam and Eve was not in their nakedness, but in the realization that they were separate and had not learned how to love in order to redeem their union. As mentioned earlier, it is the pain of unresolved separation that is the source of much of our anxiety and the quest for its resolution by effective communication is the way that conflict is solved.

As pointed out again by John Powell *"it is a simple truth that if you want to be loved, you have to be lovable. To be lovable you must love, forgive, understand, listen, be just and indulgent."* These are some of the core qualities of communication.

Let us profile once again a rare type of person that many of us have occasionally met, known and admired. They can be of either gender, any age, and from any social or cultural group. One thing they have in common however, is an uncanny ability to get along with people and in so doing they often float through life with an envied ease and calm.

In the workplace, for example, they have the ear of management and are respected by their subordinates because they listen, interact and make their opinions known in the right areas.

Management equally respects them because they have a feel for the issues and concerns of the staff and have a sensitive well-tuned ear to the dynamics of the organization. They are rarely subject to, or are the victims of, the vagaries of office politics or gossip, and although their opinions are not always universally approved, they are always listened to and respected.

These individuals believe intuitively that their success depends primarily on their relationship with others. A relationship which is maintained by their being, by nature, effective communicators.

By acting in this way these individuals wield a subtle and almost magical influence on their immediate environment, an influence that cannot be readily identified with charm, power or appearance.

They are in fact contemporary masters of four very special and almost magical arts that I describe in detail in my book *"The Art of Effective Living"* and can be regarded as the core skills of communication and are briefly described as follows:

1. The magical art of dealing with conflict.

This involves understanding that conflict, irrespective of whether it is among individuals, organisations or nations, arises because of a real or perceived loss of value, power or influence. Individuals who understand this know how to recognise this and to return it.

2. The magical art of pleasing.

This does not involve paying false compliments in order to drag others into your own sphere of influence. It does however involve believing that there is a spark of gold in everyone. Individuals who realise this, wait patiently until they find it and then tell the other that they have done so. In doing so, they give the greatest gift possible, that of self-esteem. Three hundred years ago Lord Chesterfield in "Letters to my son" made the wise comment which is as relevant then as now.

"Make a man like himself and he will become your disciple forever. Your job is to make those who are indifferent to you into your friends and your friends into even greater ones because in life no one can really afford one real enemy."

The intention however is not to create disciples but to create an environment that enhances survival.

3. The magical art of grace.

This is a very subtle quality that expresses an individual's deep belief in civilised and rational behaviour. People who practice the art of grace believe that as a species, we possess superior qualities that allow us (if we choose) to appreciate the finer aspects of human life, morality and ethics and which enable us to plan for more durable and progressive means of survival.

4. The magical art of communication.

Effective communication with the people around you is a vital factor in creating an authentic self.

It is also the key to success in work and in all social interactions.

Effective commination skills are essential in establishing authentic, loving and life-enhancing relationships. It is also equally true that ineffective communication skills create will create bad ones.

You need effective communication skills and strategies to share ideas and experiences, to find out about things that interest you, to explain to people who you are, what you want and to express your feelings. Effective communication is the way you bridge the gap between the reality of your inner self and that of the outside world and to fuse them both into a functioning whole. The alternative is a separate, conflicting and often painful divide.

If you communicate effectively with the people around you, *you'll begin to proactively shape, mould and to manipulate your world as you wish it to be, and to the extent that you can. If you do not, it will shape you and usually to your disadvantage.*

Effective communication in all of its areas involves four components and if any of these are missing you are not really communicating.

The four essential components of effective communication

1. Initial transmission of information

There is often a tendency in close relationships to feel that the *"other side"* has magical powers of of insight and should know what you think or feel. It would be nice if this were the case. Most people however are too involved with their own feelings and problems to be overly sensitive to yours. If you want to transmit information do so *intentionally and clearly* and not as often happens in an oblique manner in order to frequently manipulate.

2. Receipt of that information

It is not sufficient to merely transmit information. It is also vitally important to ensure that it is received. A husband or wife who constantly *"tune out"* their spouse by nagging or complaining, a speaker or teacher who is boring or a communicator who lacks the ability to grasp their audience's attention may well be transmitting information but it is not being effectively received.

3. Receiver's understanding of the sender's Message

The purpose of communication is for people to understand the information being sent. Are you being too technical or complicated? Are you speaking at the intellectual, social, cultural and linguistic level of your audience? are you trying to be elitist, pompous or too professorial? are you trying to impress or to inform.

These are the questions an effective communicator should regularly ask of themselves. Cultural differences can be more profound than you suspect. Members of some cultures may well react with total embarrassment and even shame at being told quite gently that they have annoyed you. Others may not react at all until your irritation is expressed more strongly. A complex concept may be explained easily to someone educated in it, but someone else may need a much more graphic and yet simpler explanation.

In other words, how are you transmitting your message?

4. Acknowledgement by the receiver that they understand the sender's message.

How can you know that *your* message has been understood? So that you can progress further. Quite simply you ask and clarify. You watch for appropriate body language and above all you listen. Effective listening is the most powerful tool in the arsenal of communication. When you listen effectively while using the appropriate body language you begin to fully understand the other person.

However, at an equally effective level you increase their self-esteem by valuing what they say, confirming that their message has been received and understood, acknowledging their communication skills and encouraging their desire to do so. As the English writer Sydney Smith wittingly suggested two hundred years ago: *"the ability to speak several languages is a valuable asset, but to be able to hold your tongue is one is priceless"*

The Role of Empathy

There is no doubt that an essential pre-condition in developing communication skills is empathy. However, the question is often asked whether this is an inherent part of our basic make up, or whether it can be developed as part of our own on-going survival needs.

This question is somewhat more complicated in that although we start this life with basic communication skills, empathy does not seem to be one of them and would seem to be something we develop in order to enhance our survival.

A new born baby and young children are rarely empathic to the needs of their parents and in fact very often not at all. Were they to continue into their adult life while only maintaining the dynamics of that early relationship their social progress as adults would be severely limited. So, it would seem that although basic communication skills are inherent, more important ones come later.

Before looking more closely at empathy however, let us look first at a few other words that seem to be similar but which are substantially different. These are pity, sympathy and compassion.

PITY

Pity does not usually go down well with those who are being pitied because it is essentially subjective and somehow demeaning and condescending. It often implies a kindly but internal regret or sadness aroused by the suffering of others. This can often lead to a demonstration of mercy, it is however, almost always subjective relating to the one who is pitying rather than the one being pitied. Pity does not go down well with most people, much less those who have a disability as it often seems to imply that they are seen as inferior, lacking or deficient in some way and that negates their basic humanness. Pity can often be self-indulgent which often leads to a lack of desire to really help.

SYMPATHY

Sympathy is closer to the concept of empathy in that it suggests a general affinity with another's negative situation and a desire to comfort. Where this differs is that there is no real intentional understanding and any emotional involvement is not so genuine, intense or personally felt. Having sympathy for another's negative situation does not typically involve going out of your way to help them. For instance, you may feel sympathy and genuine regret for someone who is sick or elderly but do not necessarily feel the need to help with their shopping or hospital trips.

EMPATHY

Empathy involves an intentional effort to understand and participate in the emotional, mental and physical situation of the other. In regular communication it involves genuinely seeing, or trying to see the situation from their perspective. True communication at its highest level is not possible unless it is realised that this is an *"a priori"* pre-condition because all people have an opinion both of their situation and the world. An opinion that has nothing to do with intelligence or culture.

In dealing with someone who is in a seriously negative situation. Empathy goes one step deeper, in that although you may have a great deal of sympathy you will never truly understand until you genuinely try to feel the limitations that condition implies. Many years ago, a very good friend who had recently arrived from South Africa during the apartheid period told me wisely that you may sympathise with the black population in South Africa and may have genuine compassion for their plight but you will never really understand it unless you intentionally try to feel the daily limitations on their humanity that apartheid imposed. He proceeded to give me many examples of those limitations.

You may have both sympathy and compassion for a paraplegic confined to a wheel chair but you can never really communicate fully until you consider how they

get up to go to the toilet at night, who they ask, what happens if their wheel chair topples over and how they even cook.

True communication does not involve forcing yourself into these positions, but it does involve trying to fully understand them.

COMPASSION

Compassion *"implies a deep sympathy for the sorrows or troubles of another coupled to a powerful urge to alleviate the pain or distress or to remove its source."* This does not necessarily involve understanding but could certainly involve attempting to fix another's problem in order to make that other person's life easier and not out of any desire for personal gain.

CONCLUSION

We cannot control the behaviour of others or the beliefs that lead to them, but we can always control how we respond to them. It is the degree of that response that is the core of communication.

CHAPTER TWO

The Essential Basics of Communication

Major communication tools…
What you want to do, communicate and achieve …
Communication in leadership.

"Developing excellent communication skills is absolutely essential to effective leadership. The leader must be able to transmit a sense of urgency, commitment and enthusiasm to others. If they cannot do this, they should be content to follow"

Gilbert Amelio.
President and CEO of
National Semiconductor Corp.

"You can learn communication skills. It's like riding a bicycle or typing. If you're willing to work at it, you can rapidly improve the quality of your life by improving them"

Brian Tracy

"One important thing in communication is observing what isn't being said. The art of reading between the lines is a lifelong quest of the wise"

Shannon L. Adler

Major communications tools.

Given that communication skills are an essential component of an effective and satisfying life. A relevant question is: can they be learned or are we born with these basic skills? The key here is basic. Yes, we are generally born with the basic skills as discussed earlier but basic skills are generally not enough for enhanced survival. They have to be developed and improved to face the ongoing and frequently changing challenges of life.

Is this difficult to do and do we have to be constantly aware of the need to practice them? The simplistic, but never the less correct answer is yes, it can be difficult. But the difficulty is similar to that we found when learning to walk, tying our shoelaces or subsequently driving a car. However, there comes a time, often far sooner than later that it becomes an automatic part of our behaviour.

Most people when they have driven to work in the morning would be hard-put to remember how many stop lights they passed or even the traffic conditions because their actions were automatic. The same goes for communication. The key is awareness which rapidly leads to effective communication becoming a general and automatic part of your life style.

An initial approach to developing this is to study what good communicators do. These skills can perhaps be summarised as:

- *They know what they want to say*
- *They know how to get the attention of the listener*
- *They know how to maintain that attention*

- *They are active and pro-active listeners*
- *They know how to observe and understand verbal and non-verbal feedback.*

The five major steps in effective communication

(1) The way you speak
(2) The words you use
(3) The body language you adopt
(4) How your words are affecting your audience
(5) Knowing what you want to communicate and achieve.

Let us have a brief look at each of these in turn.

(1) The Way you speak.

This is often determined by the needs of the audience and the speaking environment. Do you speak at the appropriate volume and speed?

One-on-one conversations can be quieter than in a larger setting. Elderly people may need you to speak at a higher volume. Those whose mother tongue is different may well understand you perfectly if the words are pronounced more slowly and with more emphasis.

Only about 50% - 60% of meaning rests in the words that are used. The rest is determined by how they are used, your body language, and the pitch, tone, emphasis, and melody you put into your voice.

Think for a moment of the differences in meaning that can be implied by tone and emphasis on the following request. *"Please pass me the butter."* It could easily range from a command to a friendly request, anger, sarcasm of courtesy. The difference being where the emphasis is placed:

Will you pass **me** the butter? *(me, and no one else)*
Will **you** pass me the butter? *(you, and no one else)*
Will you pass me the **butter**? *(not the sugar)*
Will you pass me the butter? (I've asked you twice)

SELF TEST

To demonstrate the importance of word emphasis, try the following exercise on your friends and note the probable response.

*"You make me angry when
you never phone and only email"*

"You make me angry when you
never phone and only email"
*"Sorry, but sometimes I do phone.
In fact, I phone quite a lot"*

"**You** make me angry when
you never phone and only email.
*I'm the only one? So, no one else
ever makes you angry?*

"You make me **angry** when
you never phone and rely on email"
*You get angry over such little things.
Why don't you grow up?*

"You make me angry when
you never phone and **only** rely on email"
Hey! Give me a break. I write, visit and text.

"You make me angry when
you never phone and rely on email"
*So everyone else phones? What about
your Mum she hasn't phoned this year?*

Each one of these are likely to elicit a negative
response. The following will probably not:

"I wish you would phone more.
Email is not quite the same"

I know you love email but can you
call a bit more as I miss speaking to you.

My email has gone crazy.
Can you phone instead of texting?

(2) The words you use and how you use them.

Your words do not create your listener's actions but
they do evoke the emotions that lead to them. How do
you speak? what is your body language saying? what
emotions are your words going to likely evoke in your
listener? are they accurate reflections of both what you
want to say and want to achieve? Let us look at an
example.

Your companion regularly arrives late when you have an appointment and this irritates you. In telling them of your irritation it is important to ask yourself what you want to achieve and which of the following are likely to do so.

You can say. *"You really make me annoyed when you arrive late, would you see if you can be more on time?"*

It is quite likely that this will create an immediate defensive response. Why is this? The other person knows sub-consciously that it is a lie. They cannot *"make you angry"* because they cannot operate the emotional system that makes you do so. Only neuro surgeons can do that. However, they are not able to challenge the lie and will often become defensive.

Alternately you could say. *"You know every time you arrive late, I get irritated. I don't want to because it's likely to spoil our evening together"*

It is far less likely they will get annoyed for the simple reason it is a straight forward statement of fact that they are unable to refute.

(3) The Body language you adopt.

Very early in our human development and before the development of language body language was the essential way of communicating. It is only with the development of language as we know it today that the importance of body language diminished, being replaced by the spoken word. However, it is still vitally important, operating as it does, to convey our opinion, emotion, and attitude at a less obvious and generally sub-conscious level.

In fact, next to listening, it may well be the second most vital of our communicative skills.

It is suggested that when understanding and then practicing body language the following should be noted:

- *Eye contact.* This is substantially different from staring. This tells the other person that your attention is on them, on their person and their words.

In doing so it reinforces their significance in the conversation. Eye contact is often matched by subtle body language which can convey interest understanding, suspicion and many other emotions. Just staring does not do so and is easily discernible by the subject being stared at.

To observe the difference, see if you can practice the following exercise, although after it, see if you can advise the subject what you were doing.

SELF TEST

When next in conversation with someone decide to look at them with a fixed stare but with no accompanying body language or emotion. You will detect very quickly by their body language and very often verbally as well that they are uncomfortable.

On another occasion and preferably with another subject make solid eye contact but accompany it by one of the following emotions:

- suspicion re the truth of what they are saying -
- intense concentration on their words -
- admiration for them as a person -

> *In each instance be aware of the slight changes in the body language you are displaying to reinforce that emotion and how it actually reinforces it. i.e., mouth, eyes, posture, position of hands re the face, arms folded or open. It is these subtle but definitive distinctions that the other person observes and interprets.*
>
> *Also observe any changes in their body language in response.*

- *Smile.* A genuine smile is magical. When you smile at someone it is generally about you and is an expression of your positive emotions. It is your way of saying *"I feel good."* However, as soon as it is released it changes shape and when it is received is then about the receiver and tells them that you feel good about seeing them.

It is what I often refer to as one of our magical tools of communication. However, it must be genuine and not just a hook to manipulate. Human instinct is often infallible in this area and is quickly detected.

- *Keep a posture which expresses your feelings and emotions.* As mentioned earlier it is imperative that we express our emotions and feelings as it is only then that others can really get to know us. If we don't we are hiding behind a facade which at best reduces our ability to communicate but which at worst destroys it completely. It is our frequently sub-conscious body language which gives us the tools to do so.

"I'm not sure I believe you"

Note the thoughtful position of the hands and the serious expression.

"I'm not really interested"

Note the closed arms, slouching posture, bored look and facial expression

"I'm not really interested"

Note the closed arms, slouching posture, bored look and facial expression

Would you buy a used car from this guy?

"I've read the book on eye-contact. I hope it works" Note the glassy stare which is not allied to an obvious emotion. He could well be on the beach in Florida.

"We are in complete agreement and understanding. It's a pleasure doing business with you"

Note the sincere smile, open relaxed posture and eye contact.

Obviously, this guy is a grandmaster of the art of communication and needs no lessons.

- *Show that you are thinking about the other person's words.*

Lean forward, narrow your eyes as if thinking, nodding.

- *Emphasise by facial expression that you understand and are in agreement and also watch for the other person's body language response.*

- Make sure that your posture and facial expressions reflect how you feel.

- *Smile (if appropriate to the occasion).*

Your body language MUST be an authentic expression of how you feel, negative or positive otherwise there is no real communication.

(4) How your words affect your audience.

Irrespective of whether your audience is one on one, a small group, or an auditorium they will let you know very quickly the effect your words are having on them. They may not do this intentionally and may not be aware that they are even doing so.

- One-on-one conversations.

Eye contact: *Is your listener looking at you, through you, or away from you?*

Reaction: *How are they responding? Head nodding, facial reactions, surprise.*

Interrupting: *Are they interrupting before you finish a sentence or obviously waiting for you to do so?*

Questions: *Are they asking relevant questions or just listening to your monologue?*

Clarification: *Do they ask for clarification?*

Posture: *Are they leaning forward in an obviously listening pose, arms folded, sitting comfortably or slouching?*

- Groups.

It is equally important to be aware of a group's reaction to your speaking style. With however, a couple of additional points.

Talking to a companion: *Are they talking to a companion while you are speaking?*

Doodling: *Are they making notes or otherwise trying to pass the time until you have finished? In the former they will generally keep glancing up so as not to miss what you are saying.*

Coughing: *This is a definite give away. If people are interested, they will generally do their best to refrain from coughing. For some reason there is not the same restraint when they are bored.*

Eye-contact: *Are they looking at you?*

Reaction: *How do they respond? Head nodding, facial reactions, surprise, laughter.*

Questions: *When appropriate, are they asking relevant questions or just listening to your monologue?*

By developing instinctive observation skills and awareness you can quickly detect if your subject or group is interested, bored, impatient, lacking in interest, inspired or unable to follow. The effective communicator knows at which point to adjust their style.

(5) Knowing what you want to do, communicate and achieve

We can never really communicate unless we know what we want to do, communicate and achieve.

These are vitally important because they involve self-understanding, both of our motives, goals and personality and more importantly how this will achieve our deeper goals.

Is our goal based on our deeper need to coexist, and relate with our environment or is it motivated by a desire to prove something, manipulate or win? The latter may well be the antithesis of the others and may indeed destroy them.

When you communicate you must generally have an overall aim in mind. Even light-hearted conversation is backed by a goal.

Each of these require various sub-goals which are adjusted as the interaction progresses and you will need to use specific skills to achieve them. Let us look at some of the many goals that you may have:

<u>Informative:</u> *This seeks to increase a person's knowledge and to encourage independent thinking.*

Key points are:
- *Don't be a know all. Accept your own knowledge limitations.*
- *Accept disagreement with good grace.*
- *Respect their cultural background.*
- *Ensure that the information given relates to their issues and not just an opportunity for you to display your wisdom.*

<u>Supportive:</u> *This seeks to affirm a person's self-worth and value and encourages them to realise the validity of their opinions, attitudes and feelings.*

Key points are:
- *Empathy.*

<u>Understanding:</u> *This seeks to establish a uniformity of thought and an understanding of the other person's point of view. It does not imply agreement but merely a sincere understanding of the parameters surrounding their opinion.*

Key points are:
- *Proactive listening.*

<u>Cooperative:</u> *This seeks to obtain the other persons support in fulfilling a mutual goal.*

Key points are:
- *proactive enquiry and focussing on mutual goals and benefits.*

Persuasion: *This seeks to encourage someone to agree with you.*

Key points are:
- *Pro-active listening to gain an understanding of the other's position.*
- *Present their opinions, arguments and attitudes first and if possible, proceed to challenge them with superior logic.*
- *If you cannot do that, are you prepared to withdraw without bullying, raising your voice or using irrational logic?*

Confrontation: *Involves letting the other person know that you are not in agreement with them, explaining your reasons and making suggestions for resolution. This is often the most demanding skills.*

Key points:
- *Understanding the level at which the other person is reacting, emotional, logical or illogical.*
- *A realisation that confrontation and conflict generally arise from loss of value or power.*
- *Proactive appreciation and an expressed understanding of their anger.*
- *Clarity in explaining your position while appreciating theirs, but not negating yours.*
- *Expressed willingness to compromise.*
- *Ability to use the power of words to give back any perceived loss of value, power or influence.*

- Ability to transfer an emotional level to a rational and thinking one.

Try the following self-test as it may apply to the six categories: informative, supportive, understanding, co-operative, persuasive and confrontive.

TEST YOURSELF

Take at least three of the above categories and assess your strengths and weaknesses. In which categories do you need to develop your skills and why? We suggest: Confrontive, Persuasive, Informative.

Do you use any of these in a manipulative, compulsive way or one that hinders your growth? You can improve these skills by relating them to your own relationships. Many people find these three are significant.

Confrontive. Are your own emotions obstructing the situation? Are you more interested in winning than reducing conflict? How significant is the "problem?" Have you really tried to understand?

Persuasion. Have you tried to look at the validity of your opinions or have your emotions hindered you? Have you made it clear that you understand and appreciate the other person's opinion? Obviously they have one. Remember having an opinion has nothing to do with intellect, or emotional stability.

Informative. Are you teaching, informing, advising, impressing or helping? Have you ascertained what the listener needs, expects or hopes for?

Communication in leadership.

Often and in each of our lives many of us are thrust, often unwillingly, into a position of leadership. It may be as a result of personal ambition, a significant promotion in the work place, as part of our community activity or merely as a result of growing by age and seniority into the leadership of a family or group. This involves a significant responsibility, as it is the leader who ultimately moulds and guides the attitudes, culture and morality of the group.

Effective leadership, if indeed it is to be effective, involves many interdependent qualities. These include vision, harmony with the needs of the group, a perceived sense of advanced skills, self-confidence and consistency.

In populist political leaders this often involves ensuring that the "vision" of the group is greater than individual personal obligation, a subject however which is beyond the scope of this book. Let us look at each of these in detail and how effective communication techniques can create and enhance them.

(1) Vision.

To be followed, leaders must have a clear goal to which their actions are directed. The leader's personal goals may not be always benevolent but they must be perceived as such. This demands effective communication skills that enable them to communicate with those who they require to follow.

(2) Harmony with the needs of the group.

The effective leader must use their communication skills to ascertain the needs of the group they lead, to let them know that they have done so and to harmonise their actions to meet those goals and those of the group and organisation. This is achieved not only by talking but more importantly by listening, enquiring, watching and observing.

There are both group and organisational goals but there are also individual ones. The ability to recognise all three and where possible to harmonise them is an essential skill of an effective leader.

Let us look at how these might apply to the challenges of the manager of a small direct reporting staff. For them the group's needs may well to be seen as part of an efficient and well-respected group within an organisation, that the future security of the group is a significant goal and that the leader is trusted to represent their communal interest.

On the other hand, individual needs that should be recognised could be a younger person's ambition, extra training or for promotional ones, a young mother's need for a greater flexibility in terms of time schedules or someone in a junior position for more interesting work. One individual may need encouragement, another understanding and another active assistance, but in each case listening, watching, asking the right questions and sensitivity are key. A leader's goal is to do their best to accommodate these different desires. Not all may be achievable or even compatible, but knowing what they are and knowing how to fuse them is essential.

(3) A perceived sense of advanced skills.

In our continuing study of communication in leadership we come to an area that is often the most difficult to describe as it can hint at elitism which it is not. It begs the simple question *"why should I follow you?"* and *"why should I not be the leader with its perceived but often illusory benefits?"*

The simple answer is that the leader should be seen as having some qualities that are generally admired. It is up the leader to communicate that awareness in a way that enforces that belief but at the same time is neither arrogant, elitist or self-aggrandising.

In a business setting for example these skills could include being a recognised specialist in the job at hand, emotional objectivity, being able to give credit to a subordinate without being threatened by their competence, having a sense of what fair play really means, self-confidence, vision or a superior understanding of the issues. There are many more and it is certainly not possible to be top of the class in all or even most of them. However at least some must be able to answer the question *"why should I follow you?"* It is the leader's communicative skills that reinforces that awareness.

In summary the leader should not strive to be an equal. This involves being separate from the group but at the same time a significant part of it.

(4) Self-confidence.

Leaders use their communication skills to convey a feeling of personal trust in their own abilities, qualities, and judgment.

This self-confidence implies a basic positive belief in their skills and abilities. It means that they accept, respect and trust themselves and their basic instincts and have a strong sense of control in the management of their life.

Effective leaders are aware of their strengths and weaknesses however, and can handle criticism without it affecting their self-esteem. This allows them to set realistic expectations both of themselves and others. Effective leaders communicate this in the following ways:

- they are prepared to let others know how they think and feel and are not averse to defending both even though this may not be universally accepted.

- they do not specifically court popularity but do not go out of their way to avoid it.

- they are prepared to take calculated risks having confidence in their basic judgment of the risk involved.

- they have specific ideas of their needs, wants and interests, let others know of it and actively pursue them.

(5) Consistency.

Consistency is a major key to success as a leader. This is communicated by focusing both on the current task at hand while maintaining the consistency and regularity of a long-term observable goal.

This gives security to those who follow, as this is an inherent human need and allows the group to feel secure in the direction that the group is taking. They may not necessarily agree with that direction or be in full support of it but this is usually overcome by their confidence in the leader's commitment. When a leader does something consistently both currently and in terms of their vision, they receive feedback in terms of agreement and support. This reaffirms the leader's goal which enables them to confidently change direction when circumstances require it.

In the workplace this creates a favourable work environment characterized by trust, productivity and a feeling of security. In the family or community, it reinforces and encourages the moral, social and cultural ethos which each community requires.

CHAPTER 3
Listening

Effective listening and its importance...Listening versus hearing... Four steps to effective listening.

Listening can be regarded as one of the most vital skills in communication. Unfortunately, however, it is usually the one that is most neglected.

Listening is far more than just hearing. Hearing is an automatic and physical function of the hearing system. Even when we are not doing so consciously, we hear sounds around us every day. Traffic outside our window, the clock ticking, people talking in the next room. It is only when we purposely pay attention to those sounds that we are actively listening and this implies an intentional decision to decode sound and to give it meaning. The more we do this, the greater our communication skills become.

Exercise in Listening

One of the earliest steps in developing listening skills is to watch and honestly observe yourself the next few times you have a regular conversation, preferably by telephone.

Make a sincere attempt to act as you would normally do and without any hidden motive. This is easy when you realise that effective, and more frequently ineffective listening is a habit that will not break overnight just because we are trying to observe it.

- how often do you get distracted, from listening?

- how often are their words reflected back internally as part of your experience rather than the speaker's?

- do you often wait for a break in the conversation to continue your observations? and more significantly,

- how often are you tempted to interrupt and finish the speaker's sentences before they do?

- how often does that response start with "I" and a personal statement rather than a deeper probe into the speaker's position?

The big question is why do we do this.

Why are people poor listeners?

Few of us are good listeners. Those who are, are generally more effective communicators and subsequently have stronger and more meaningful relationships.

- You are not trained to listen. Listening is a skill that is not inherent but which can be learned. In our childhood we tend to talk more in order to bring attention to ourselves. Maturity should lessen the need for this.

- You are not attending to the person speaking due to lack of interest or personal distraction.

- You usually make premature interpretations and judgments.

- You interrupt generally because you believe your comments and opinions are more important.

- You prepare your reply while the speaker is speaking.

- You often hear what you want, hope or expect to hear.

- You immediately and subjectively personalise your response.

If you are doing any of the above, you are not only missing the real, deep or often hidden meaning in the speaker's message but as importantly are devaluing them and their significance in the conversation.

Let us look at a typical conversation from these two perspectives.

John has just lost his job. He has been given a plausible reason but does not really believe it so he discusses it with his friend Jim, a non-listener.

John: How are you doing Jim?

Jim: Not bad. What's up Buddy?

John: To be honest I'm a bit stressed out. I was laid off on Friday.

Jim: Wow! That's tough. That happened to me some years ago. Pain in the butt and quite worrying.

41

John: Yes, I'm quite concerned as you know I've got a heavy mortgage and debts. My wife's - - -

Jim: I bet she's worried. Mine was until we got it sorted out. Why did they fire you?

John: Well. Bill, the general manager ---

Jim: That guy, you always said he was a jerk.

John: I know, he just called me in and said for economic reasons he had to say good-bye.

Jim: That's crazy man, you're the best salesman they have. I wouldn't accept it. Can you go to the union or get a lawyer?

John: Well - I was thinking of it but ----

Jim: I know, they are expensive but in the long run it might be worth it.

I'm not sure, but thanks for listening.

However, John is not satisfied and phones his older brother Pete who has been round the block a few times.

John: How you doing Pete?

Pete. Not bad. What's up Buddy.

John: To be honest I'm a bit stressed out. I was laid off on Friday.

Pete: Wow! That's tough. What happened?

John: Yeh, I'm quite concerned, as you know I've got a heavy mortgage and a few debts. My wife's worried about it.

Pete: Look, I know Jean from old, she's tough, she'll rise to the occasion. Why did they fire you?

John: Bill, the general manager called me in and told me I had to go because of economic reasons.

Pete: Do you believe him?

John: Well, we have had several disagreements about procedural stuff and he's not the kind of guy who likes to be challenged. I also thought the company was in good financial shape.

Pete: Look John, we both know you have far superior knowledge about the job. My guess is that he feels threatened. He's not a bad guy and I am sure he'll give you a good reference. With your qualifications I think you can get another job easily. Especially given the reasons for the lay-off.

John: Do you really think so?

Pete: No doubt about it. Maybe in the long run parting company may not be such a bad idea. What do you think?

John: Maybe this is the opportunity I should have taken years ago. I've not been overly happy there for a while.

Pete: A friend of mine at the club is a top-level recruiter would you like me to speak to him?

John: Yes, that would be great. Thanks Pete see you soon.

In the first of these conversations, it is clear that Jim is not really interested in listening. He interrupts frequently in anticipation of what he thinks is going to be said and tries to bounce each statement back to his own perspective rather than delving further into the conversation itself. Pete, on the other hand listens fully without interrupting or interpreting, tries to get deeper explanations by asking open ended questions and based on them is able to give practical comments.

Four Major Steps to Effective Listening.

1. Face the speaker, maintain eye contact and be attentive.

In most cultures, though certainly not all, eye contact is regarded as a basic ingredient of good listening. Try to look rather than stare. A few moments trying both will easily identify the body language of each.

Try to set aside anything thing that might distract you i.e., papers, books and telephone and mentally screen out distractions such as background activity and other noise.

Try to also control the distractions of your own thoughts and focus on the feeling that this is their time as well as yours.

2. Keep an open mind and ask open questions.

Listen without judging the other person or their motives. There may come a time for that, but it is not really possible until you have listened to them. Remember that the speaker is using language to represent the thoughts and feeling that are happening in their head and not yours. Yours can only ever be an interpretation of their thoughts.

Try to avoid interrupting their sentences mid-way as the chances are, they will feel cheated out of their opportunity to express themselves. In addition, and as you will be following your train of thought you will usually be wrong and totally off base.

Try not to seek an opportunity to use their words to change the conversation direction i.e.

Anne: "Last week I went to the Doctor as I wasn't feeling too well and bumped into Janet"

Maria: "You did? I haven't seen her since we both went to the theatre and saw 'Les Misérables.' How was she?"

Anne: "Fine. She's moving to Vancouver with Bill's new job"

Maria: "Nice place - have you ever been there?"

Anne: "Yes, I liked it. So, what will Bill be doing there?"

Maria: "Something to do with mining I think"

Light hearted banter like this is fine and usually part of regular conversation. However, care should be taken that you are not the one constantly changing direction. Maybe Anne really wanted to talk about her doctor's visit.

This particular conversational affront happens quite frequently. One question leads in a direction that may have nothing to do with where either thought they were going or even wanted to go. Sometimes we end up going back to the original topic but not often.

Use open ended questions. How, when, where, why, what and tell me about. These are truly amazing skills for encouraging listening and conversation. In talking with someone they are the main ingredients of almost all communicative conversation and are often quite magical in their effect. They are questions that require more than just a yes or no answer.

In the previously mentioned conversations above between John, Jim and Pete you will notice that Jim only used one open question but Pete used four and was obviously far more adept at understanding the situation and helping.

3. Listen to the speaker's words and try to feel what they are feeling.

Pay attention to what isn't said – to non – verbal clues. When you are paying attention to the speaker and focusing on them you will quickly detect enthusiasm, boredom, irritation, surprise or genuine interest. These can be observed by the way they are sitting, whether they are focusing on you, the set of the mouth, expression around the eyes and the pacing, pausing and emphasis of their words.

Empathy is the heart and soul of good listening. It involves actively trying to understand the speaker's feelings and attitude *from their point of view and not your own.*

Empathy involves an intentional effort to understand and participate in the emotional, mental and physical situation of the other. In regular communication it involves genuinely seeing, or trying to see, the situation from their perspective. True communication at its highest level is not possible unless it is realised that this is an *"a priori"* pre-condition because all people have an opinion both of their situation and the world. An opinion that has nothing to do with intelligence, culture or training.

Allow your mind to create a mental image of the information being conveyed Your brain will automatically do this if you remain focused with senses fully alert. Watch carefully for their body language as it reinforces their spoken words.

When listening try not spend the time planning what to say next in response, as you cannot easily listen and rehearse your next act at the same time. If you feel congruent emotions when the other person expresses theirs your effectiveness as a listener is assured.

Wait for the Speaker to pause to ask clarifying questions instead of interrupting with your own opinions or solution.

4. Give regular feedback

Show that you understand where the speaker is coming from by reflecting their "expressed" feelings. *"You must have really enjoyed that" – "That must have been a shock to you"* but try to avoid saying *"I fully understand how you feel"* or words to that effect. You cannot "know" how they feel and only very rarely will you be actually *"in their shoes."* Often this can tend to belittle their experience.

However, be prepared to occasionally interject (not interrupt) with expressions such as "uh-uh" "hmmm" or "wow" as appropriate to the dialogue.

CHAPTER 4
Using Communication Skills to Resolve Conflict

What is conflict?... Causes of conflict... Return of power... Reinforcing value...Using communication skills to resolve conflict.

WHAT IS CONFLICT?

Differences of opinion are a normal and healthy part of human relations. By resolving our differences in a reasoned and rational manner we evolve into a new understanding both of the individuals involved and of the situation under disagreement. This obviously enhances both our wisdom and our capacity to communicate.

Within our common understanding of the word however, conflict frequently and sadly involves another factor, namely the emotions, and the emotion is often controlled irritation, anger, or at best a vigorous assertion of one's own previously expressed opinion. *We get angry when we fear that our values, intellect or influence are under attack and that we will lose something as a result.* Sadly, this is usually the very worst reaction because it is then that we need a rational approach more than ever.

The first step in the resolution of conflict is to be aware of what is being attacked or perceived as being attacked.

It is an axion in modern psychology that when emotion and reason are in conflict emotion will always win *(Emile Coue. 1857 – 1926)*. If and when this happens the problem will generally be solved by means that frequently exclude reason to the detriment of a rational solution.

CAUSES OF CONFLICT

Conflict occurs at many levels. Certainly, among individuals, but also as history observes, between nations, organisations and the many other groups that we form. However, the reasons generally are the same.

Although there are often many apparent reasons for the anger that evokes conflict (as opposed to pure disagreement) the root cause, irrespective of whether it is at a global or personal level is generally the fear that one of the following is going to happen:

(a) Real or imagined loss of power, respect or influence.

(b) Real or imagined loss of value.

Although there are a few times in which an imagined loss of power or a loss of value are the sole causes of conflict it will often be seen that in many ways they are closely interdependent as indeed are their solutions.

We often measure our value in terms of the influence we wield and in turn the more influence we wield the more value we perceive that we have. If either of these are challenged, we will do everything we can to resist the challenge and very often this will be at the expense of reason.

GENERALLY ACCEPTED (THOUGH NOT NECESSARILY ALWAYS RECOMMENDED) WAYS OF RESPONDING TO CONFLICT

(a) Use of Power *("this is what you will do – do it")*

(b) Avoidance *("let's think about it for a while," - let's put in on next month's agenda," we'll deal with it when we really have to")*

(c) Diffusion *(use of power to achieve passive compromise, everyone gets a bit of satisfaction but no one gets enough, "we're going through a tough time of year but come the Spring it will be better")*

(d) Reestablishment of power and/or value.

Solutions based on power generally aggravate the symptoms that are causing the conflict in the first place.

Solutions based on avoidance or diffusion are generally overtaken by events which force unpalatable solutions. Solutions that could have been avoided by earlier positive and pre-emptive action.

The most powerful way of dealing with conflict is to protect and if possible, to enhance the power and or value of those affected.

SUGGESTIONS FOR GIVING BACK POWER OR VALUE

<u>Understanding.</u>

-Actively and objectively search for all the facts which govern the issue.

- Express a genuine appreciation of the other person's point of view. (they have one even though you may not agree with it, but your agreement is not the immediate issue) - Put yourself in their shoes. If you do this this you will then have the tools to deal with the major issue behind the conflict – namely loss of power and/or value.

<u>Acceptance of Value</u>

Listen and question.

Clarify the concerns of all sides of the conflict.

Put yourself temporarily on the side of the other parties to the conflict i.e.

("you know I really see your point")
("I can see that you are really annoyed but I really want to know why")

Reassert value.
("the contributions that you make in every other area are amazing but I do not fully understand this one")

("I really appreciate the amazing contributions you make but on this one I really ---")

("I usually fully understand and appreciate your opinions on everything else we discuss and they always have value but I really need further input on this one")

Reassign blame.

("I know (I am sure) there are many other factors that contribute to this")

("I'm certainly not blaming you as we all know that there are many factors contributing to this")

("I know that many of our challenges are beyond your immediate control")

Appropriate Body Language.

Smile. *Indicating that you and the listener are basically on the same side.*

Listen. *Indicating that you are trying to understand their point of view.*

Lean forward. *Indicating that you are if making a sincere effort to do so.*

Voice. *A non-emotional quiet soft voice almost always implies that reason and thinking have priority rather than the emotions. A loud and assertive voice almost always indicates the opposite or that the speaker is trying to intimidate.*

In the last section we dealt with how communication skills can be used to re-establish value. Let us now move on to the second cause of conflict namely loss of power and influence and how it too can be re-established or given back. A more effective description of this is empowerment. How can we do this?

RE-ESTABLISHMENT OF PERSONAL POWER (EMPOWERMEMNT)

<u>Pro-active Compromise.</u>

"You guys are experienced members of my staff.
You know the issues so I'm relying on each of you to work
out a solution that is acceptable to you all."

<u>Transfer of Power.</u>

"What would you like me to do?"
"This is what you can do"
"Have you considered?"
"Come up with a solution and I'll go for it"
"I think that many of John's ideas have merit"
"I wonder if you can help me?"
"What would you suggest?"

SOME EXAMPLES OF CONFLICT AND SUGGESTED SOLUTIONS

(1)

Manager gets irritated when an employee keeps disagreeing with them or comes up with alternatives to their decisions. The employee on the other hand does not think that the manager has thought the situation through and is possibly not experienced enough to do so. If a situation like this is not resolved it generally works to the disadvantage of both.

Suggestion.

<u>From the mangers point of view.</u>

The employee probably does not think that their opinions are valued (loss of value). The manager should make it clear that the employee is an important part of the organisation (section/division) and that their skills are highly regarded. They should ask the employee to describe some of their major concerns (not how the manager has made wrong decisions) and should then make a serious and objective attempt to understand them. Even to the extent of commenting "I hadn't considered that aspect. Thanks for pointing it out."

In a group setting this can be even more beneficial as it makes it clear that the boss has not cornered the market in wisdom and is prepared to admit it. Most individuals appreciate this quality in a leader and those who do not are perhaps not worth worrying about. Ask the employee for alternative suggestions while not being averse to pointing out any defects in those suggestions. This is of course where verbal communication skills are invaluable.

"I think you are wrong"
can easily be replaced by
"but, have you thought what would happen if ----?"

"I strongly disagree"
can easily be replaced by
*"I am really not sure if I fully agree
on all the points here"*

and of course, the highly dangerous:

"Don't tell me my job"
can easily be replaced by
"I really appreciate your input.
It makes my job so much easier."

From the employee's point if of view.

Very similar skills are needed whilst realising that the manager is probably (possibly) being motivated by loss of power rather than the employee's loss of value. This can be trickier.

"I hope you don't mind if I put in my 2 cents worth"
or
"Have you considered?

Can easily replace

"I don't think you have thought about-----?"

"I will of course do what you say,
you're the chief but I do have some reservations."

Can easily replace

"I don't think I can follow your instructions here"

"A private discussion is often more appropriate than a group one where a manager's authority can easily be compromised.

Yes, much of this can be regarded as manipulative but as been discussed many times earlier survival is the mother of communication.

Employees should make sure they understand the manager's position by listening objectively and asking clarifying questions. Indicate that you feel that their (the manager's) suggestions and the reason for them have merit but feel free to suggest one or two difficulties that may occur and if they have considered alternatives.

(2)

A customer complains over the phone about a defective product. The CSR advises nothing can be done. Customer gets furious (loss of power) with the CSR (loss of value).

<u>Suggestion from Customer point of view.</u>

Clearly outline your situation as reasonably but as firmly as possible.

Listen to the CSR's explanation before interrupting and continuing your tirade. Unless you understand the CSR, s point of view, explanation and limitations further real communication is fruitless.

Ask if there are any exceptions, an appeal process, whether it can be escalated, what are my options and if anything, what they can do. Use constructive statements which may return value to the CSR.

> *"I am not sure if you have the*
> *authority to solve the situation"*

NOT

*"Are you just a telephone clerk
or can you solve the problem?"*

Am I speaking to the right person?"

NOT

*"It doesn't sound as if you are the person
I should be speaking to"*

"I hope you can see my situation"

NOT

"You obviously don't understand, so let me repeat"

"I would really be grateful if you can help me."

NOT

*"You're the fifth person I have spoken to
so I doubt if you can help me"*

The situation is quite clear. What is your mission? do you as the customer want the problem solved or merely to vent your anger?

<u>From the CSR point of view.</u>

The customer is clearly frustrated at their inability to solve the problem, (loss of power). The CSR should let the customer know that within policy restraints the customer does have options (return of power) ranging from going to a senior level, complaining to a governing body or contacting the complaints line of a newspaper.

The CSR should listen fully from a non-defensive standpoint (this is not a personal attack on them or their value). Generally, empathise with the customer's feelings but not necessarily with the complaint. Even to the point of giving examples of their own frustration when faced with a similar example, thus siding with, and making an ally of the customer.

Advise that you will do your best to solve the situation as customer satisfaction is the only way their business can be retained even though there may be some difficulties in fully solving it.

Ask what the customer would accept if a full solution cannot be guaranteed (return of power). Advise if possible and as appropriate that you will get back to the customer within a specified time (and do it)

If there is still a total rejection advise the next step if possible (return of power).

(3)

A manager is required to criticise an employee's performance knowing that the employee will likely disagree and get irritated *(loss of value)*.

An interview of this nature demands prior thought and a specific focus on the mission of the interview.

Namely what is wanted to achieve and as importantly what is NOT wanted.

First the manager should approach the interview from a discussion rather than an authoritarian standpoint. Opening statements/questions could be:

"How are things going in your section re -----?"

"What do you think of our new plans to -----?"

"Do you have any ideas as to when we may go into the 2nd phase -----?"

Listen to any area of response where a positive and or constructive comment can be made and make it. When this groundwork has been laid the manager can then diplomatically launch into the real reason for the interview. The manager can then advise that there is one area of concern and then describe it in terms of things rather than feelings. Do not say:

"I get irritated when-----"

"Management get annoyed if --- "

"Other employees feel that ---"

but rather:

"I've noticed that -----"

"I would like to suggest that there are further areas of development that I would like you to consider"

"There is one area that concerns me. I would like to talk about it"

As mentioned at the beginning of this chapter, conflict which generally involves emotion rather than reason usually exists when there is a real or perceived loss of power or value or very often a combination of both. The mission of an effective communicator is to return both.

CHAPTER 5
Conversational Speaking

> *Generally... With your kids... With the boss... With the family... With a service provider.*

In the opening introduction to this book, I suggested that we need other people in order to survive and that our commitment to fulfilling that need is the key to survival. Effective communication is how we do so.

Nowhere is that commitment more imperative than in our daily relationships with the people around us.

It can be said that our relationship with others is essentially self-serving and to a limited extent this is true. However, those brought up in the tradition that unselfish behaviour is more virtuous are missing the point. *Our survival depends almost totally upon our interdependence with, and mutual support of, other people and effective communication skills are the key to that relationship.*

It is a fact that irrespective of who we are communicating with, there are several factors that are always applicable and it is these we will shortly address. It is also true that with each of our varied relationships there are different dynamics that will always apply and it is this individuality that effective communication should also address.

There is for example the relationship of a parent with their teenage child, an employee with their boss, a lover with their beloved. Each of these have a unique framework and it is this uniqueness we will look at in this chapter.

It is naive to believe that our communicative skills are so generic that *"one size fits all"* Effective communication needs an understanding that all relationships are unique but first let us look at the various factors that govern all relationships.

The major tools at your disposal in effectively communicating are:

(a) the way you speak, (b) the words you use, (c) the body language you adopt and (d) an awareness of the effect the first three tools are having on the person or group to whom you are speaking. Very often it is not what you say that matters but what the words imply and the feelings they and your body language generate. Let us look briefly at the major considerations that should occur to you when speaking and using body language.

- Think about your purpose in communicating and what you are trying to achieve by your words and actions. Are you trying to persuade, apologise, encourage, understand, motivate? All are different. What exactly do you want to achieve and will your words and body language achieve it?

- Think about the words that you use and how you use them. Only a limited amount of meaning rests in the words that you use. The rest is determined by how they are used, your body language, when you do so and the pitch, tone, emphasis and intonation of your voice. *Your words do not create your listener's actions; your words evoke the emotions that then power those actions.*

- How do you speak? In an authoritarian manner, persuasively, softly, or with empathy and understanding? What is your body language conveying? Is it saying *"I am open minded to what you are saying"* (relaxed open posture) - *"you won't get passed my opposite opinion"* (arms folded, teeth clenched, firm jaw) – *"I am eager to learn more"* (leaning forward and thoughtful)? Are your words and body language congruent? When asking a question are you focussed on their reply rather than your next question? Eye contact is a significant pointer here and lack of focus can be rapidly detected by the listener.

What emotions do you think your words are going to evoke in your listener? and most importantly, are they accurate reflections of what you want to say?

- Think of your audience and what they want, need or expect from your communication and will they understand the words you are using and your reason for using them?

Tips for Immediate Improvement

Here are some ways that you can immediately use your words, awareness and body language to improve your communication skills.

• Recognize that the need to communicate is the key to your survival and is an *"a priori"* condition of it.

• Try to see every situation from the other side. If you do not try to make an honest effort to do this you might appear to be communicating but you will not be doing so. Listening and clarifying are key to this.

There is an old North American Indian saying *"you will never really understand another unless you walk for a mile in their moccasins"*

Whilst this is of course metaphorical the implied message is not.

• Get the listener's attention. (How? Motivate, interest, entertain or emphasise). Every listener's attention is limited if you want them to listen to you, you have to get and keep their attention. There are generally, four accepted ways of doing so.

- Motivate them at an emotional level. How do your words relate to their emotional feelings, needs or aspirations? Do you use words that make them feel as opposed to think? *"You can be whatever you want to be"* will appeal to emotion, whereas *"if you plan, act and persevere"* appeals to reason."

In the words of a great French psychologist *"when emotion and reason are in conflict – emotion always wins."* This is why an inspirational speech is so often much more powerful than a reasoning one in that it mainly uses feeling words

- The second of the four recognised ways of keeping a listener's attention is to interest them. Individuals, because of their uniqueness are motivated by different interests. If you want to communicate well, see if you can appeal to that interest either implied or explicitly.

- The third way of getting and keeping attention is to amuse them. The prime motivator of human activity is to be happy and this can be interpreted as having fun, enjoying the moment and being entertained by a story, humour or experience.

- Finally, the fourth way of getting and keeping attention is by empathy and understanding because this is a pre-condition in developing communication skills. However, the question is often asked whether this is part of our basic make up or whether it can be developed as a part of our own on-going survival needs.

This question is a little complicated in that although we start our lives with basic communication skills, empathy does not seem to be one of them and seems to be something we develop in order to enhance our survival. New born babies and young children are rarely empathic to the needs of their parents and in fact very often not at all. If they continue into their adult life while maintaining that lack of empathy their social progress as adults will be severely limited.

So, it would seem that although our ability to communicate is basic to our nature, the skills upon which it depends usually come later. This is why some adults who lack empathy are regarded as immature which subtly implies that they have not really grown out of their childhood stage.

• Do not assume that you know the listener's thoughts, feelings or motivation. If in doubt, ask.

• Know what you want to say before you start talking.

• Be brief, clear and coherent.

• Know what interests the listener.

• Be interested in the world around you.

• Like people.

• Ask open-ended questions. (These are questions that cannot be answered with a "yes" or "no" and which usually begin with how, why, when, who, what, where or tell me about etc).

• Maintain congruent body language. (For example, don't say, *"I'm really interested in what you have to say,"* and then look out of the window)

• Listen, observe and clarify.

• Know how to end a conversation.

• Strive to establish personal relationships.

• Speak at your audience's social and cultural level.

The following amusing story will serve to illustrate your vital importance in the communication spectrum:

"An elderly man went to his doctor complaining that his wife had a communication problem in that whenever he spoke, she ignored him. The doctor wisely suggested that before they both come in for a discussion, the old fellow should find out if his wife was deaf. In accordance with the doctor's instruction and when she was next cooking dinner, he stood a little way behind her and asked what was for dinner. He was ignored.

Stepping closer, he repeated the question twice more and was again ignored each time. Standing right behind her now, he loudly asked once again. At last, she turned and in a loud voice exclaimed, "for the fourth time you deaf ole coot, it's chicken."

Effective communication is a loop of continuous cause and effect with you, the communicator, acting as both. Your boss, co-worker or employee may well have a communication problem. If one exists however, you should admit to yourself that you are part of the problem, are a part of the communication spectrum and the first person to look to for a solution.

Let us look first of at the relationship between a teenage child and a parent, which is often a source of conflict, and how effective communicative skills can impact upon it.

Communicating with a young adult.

It can sometimes be difficult for a loving parent to realise that children who generally need a high degree of guidance and control eventually become adults. They then generally need much less guidance and generally no control. However, how is this transition to be handled in the intervening period when they need both but to an ever-lessening degree and how do you as a parent negotiate that gradual change?

One important way is to sincerely recognise that transition. A teenager will generally know that they still need guidance and control but are generally reluctant to admit it. This need conflicts with their growing need for personal freedom, growth and the imperative that they make their own decisions. However, a lack of maturity often prevents them from recognising the reasons, so this responsibility must ultimately rest on the parent. Here are a few communicative tips that should guide your actions in this regard.

<u>Demonstrate unconditional love.</u>

Unconditional love is a gift freely given without any attached conditions. Loving someone in this way is not a contract but an unconditional gift to the person you love and made apparent by the way you speak and act.

Scott Peck in his great book *"The Road Less Travelled"* describes true love as existing *"when you are unconditionally committed to the growth of the beloved"* and John Powell the Jesuit inspirational writer writes, so very correctly suggests *"that a human being can only really grow in the soil of full acceptance"*

Simply put, it is love without strings attached, which you offer freely and which is not based on what someone does for you in return. You simply love them and want nothing more than their happiness.

In terms of communication it implies true listening, understanding and being able use appropriate words and body language to convey that understanding. It is said that love is blind, this is not true. True love, is in fact not blind, but super sighted, because it sees through the outer veneer to the real person underneath and fully accepts that reality. This is very beautifully described in the wonderful story of Rapunzel attributed to the Brothers Grimm.

Rapunzel is a beautiful woman locked away by an ugly witch. She never tries to escape, even though she can, because she is told that she is hideously ugly and as there are no mirrors in her prison, she believes it. However, one day a young man climbs up to her window looks at her and she sees in the reflection in his eyes that she is beautiful and she is then free from her self-imposed captivity.

Finally unconditional love makes it very clear that your love does not depend upon their actions *and that there is a subtle but profound difference between their actions, your opinion of their actions and your love of the person themselves.*

To a great degree, what a teenager becomes is mainly a reflection of what their environment tells them that they are. *(Chapter 7. Principles of Self-Affirmation. The Art of Effective Living – Geoff Smith)*

Avoid using: should, must and but.

Should, must and but, are perhaps three of the most subversive words in the English language and great care is advisable when using them.

'Should" and "must" imply that there is a universal law which somehow directs people's behaviour and "but" invariably negates a previous compliment.

Advising someone that they should or must do something implies that they are not only in breach of that law, but that you are not.

Instead of:

"You should have studied last night for your exam"
better to say
*"It would be a bit easier today
if you had studied last night"*

Instead of:

*"You must phone me when you
know you are coming home late"*
better to say
*"I really worry when you come in late.
Can you phone me next time?*

Instead of:

*"Your school report for last semester was great
but you should try to better at Math.*
Better to say:
*Your school report was great. Your math mark
could have been a bit higher but overall,
it was fantastic. I'm really happy.*

Adjust your viewpoint.

Everyone has an opinion, especially young adults. You may not agree with that opinion but that is not really relevant to communication. What is relevant however, is that you listen pro-actively in order to understand that opinion. Listening, understanding and then asking appropriate questions is the key. Then be prepared to genuinely adjust, change or even disavow those opinions if what you hear makes it necessary. John Ruskin the British satirist and writer once wrote *"It is said that we should have the courage of our convictions. However, every tyrant and despot in history have had the courage of their convictions. What is really needed is the courage to look at those convictions and reject them if they are not rational or appropriate"*

Assume they are an adult and speak as you would another adult.

When talking to a young adult try not to talk down to them with the same sense of parental direction they needed when they were much younger. In communicating with a young adult ask yourself if you would speak to a friend, relative or work colleague in the same way. If not ask yourself what is the difference in the relationship and does that justify different behaviour. Few of us would venture to tell a colleague to tidy their desk or not to put their elbows on the lunch-time table. Why tell an 18-year-old other than perhaps as guidance rather than a command.

Take personal responsibility for your feelings.

When you say *"you make me angry when ----"* they know sub-consciously that it is a lie. No one else can make you angry (except perhaps a neuro-surgeon in an operating theatre). The problem here is that not only is it untrue but it implies that the other person has that ability and are maliciously using it.

Instead of:

"You make me angry when you leave your bedroom in a mess. You must tidy it up"

Far better

"It really upsets me when I see your untidy bedroom. I would really be happy if you would tidy it up now and again"

Don't forget the importance of humour now and then. In the above example you could add *"or I will have to feed the large animals that must be living under your bed."*

Communicating with the "Boss"

As has been said many times before effective communication is a major component of personal survival and how successfully we communicate with those around is the key to that survival. However, as also mentioned our relationships all differ and although each of them has much in common such as the need to listen and understand, they equally have significantly different dynamics.

The relationship that an employee has with their manager is a lot different from that of a young adult child, a life time partner or a friend. It is important that these different dynamics be addressed. Let us look now at communication with an employer or boss.

As there are many words to describe this relationship ranging from section leader, supervisor, project manager etc I shall use the word manager to describe any relationship where you are required to report to, and be directed by, an authority figure.

Effective communication with your manager is a key element of your eventual success, your survival in the workplace and your happiness in general. It is they who in many ways govern your career advancement and personal job satisfaction. Whether you like their style of management, competence or personality is secondary to your ability to communicate with them effectively.

Let us look at some of those areas where communicative skills will achieve this.

Do not emphasise your greater knowledge or competence.

Your manager is basically the same as you, in that they do not want their position and authority threatened. Accept this as reality. If you have a specialised knowledge that your manager relies on and which is obviously outside their expertise by all means do so because that is why you are usually employed. However, if they are similar, do so with great caution.

"Did you not think of these aspects of the program?"
Will certainly arouse a defence

"I was thinking perhaps of another approach"
will not.

There us a great difference between challenging and informing and as has been said many times before effective communication is generally about how we say things not what we are saying.

Realise and accept authority.

None of us like to be controlled as we all feel that any control is a restriction on our personal freedom. This is further reinforced by the feeling that for whatever reason the manager is "better" than us in some undetermined way and because of this has been granted special powers or privilege.

However, reality and therefore our survival rests upon our fully accepting their authority. Even the president of a large corporation and indeed of a country are both subject to the whims of the market place and the voting electorate and must communicate and react effectively.

Accept sincerely that your manager has a great influence on your life, irrespective of your personal opinion as to their competence, personality or style of management. This is your reality. Effective communication both internally and externally is how you deal with and accept that reality.

Contribute to their success

Your manager's reputation and therefore their success depends to a great degree on yours. This implies that they get credit for the success of their enterprise. If that is due to your initiative and hard work most employers will be quick to pass that on to you. Do not seek to obtain credit behind their back, going over their head for it or *"bad mouthing"* them for their lack of competence, even though you may think subjectively that it is justified.

Make no mistake your manager has friends at all levels and he or she will rapidly hear about it.

An effective suggestion is to be open in private and truly supportive publicly because your manager will hear about that as well.

Remember effective communication is the child of our basic survival instincts.

Use respectful language

This is a really obvious communication requirement with everyone with whom we relate and really needs no explanation. However, many overlook its importance. However, this is even greater with someone who can take offence and who has the authority to prejudice you in some way.

For instance, if you are criticised in some way your reply could be:

"That's the third time you have criticised me this week can I not do anything right?"

or

"No one is perfect. I do my best"

77

These would immediately lead to a confrontation or at very best a defensive reaction. Effective communicators would prefer the following.

"Sorry, I did the best I can. When you have some time perhaps you can give me some tips for improvement."

If the problems in the enterprise are due to a lack of communication (implying the manager's lack of communication), far better to say.

"Some people complain that they are not too sure of the direction we are taking"

"There are some other factors that are really important that I have to mention such as-----"

are far more effective than:

"You don't understand some of the difficulties I face in my project".

Don't take your boss's courtesy and *"friendship"* for granted

Your manager wants you to be happy. How they go about it can be a different matter. If they have any sense at all (unfortunately some do not) they will be courteous and, where appropriate to your mutual status, be personally friendly.

Do not make the common mistake however of thinking that this implies a reduction or abrogation of their authority or inability to practice it. If you come in late on several occasions for example and you are criticised, this not a breach of trust but an extension of their responsibility as your manager.

To feel that it is, is your problem and results from your lack of appreciation as to where the boundaries rest.

Communicating with family.

Communicating effectively with family and friends is extremely important because it enables them to express their needs, wants, and concerns to each other. Open and honest communication creates an atmosphere that allows this.

Communication involves more than just words. It also involves the way you say those words, their implied, hidden, explicit meaning, and your body language. If you use negative methods to communicate or avoid communicating at all, this can make matters worse and seriously affect who you later become.

Poor family communication can include gossiping, yelling, holding grudges, keeping secrets, blaming, giving the silent treatment, using ultimatums or threats or labelling someone bad, instead of their behaviour. If these problems continue, you will never feel close to your family. The way parents talk to their kids or how siblings talk to each other can impact their positive development when they become adults. Young people can also get anxiety and depression if there are still feelings of inadequacy that have never left them.

An excellent way to maintain and improve family communication is to take some time away from your busy schedule to have a family discussion. It need not be too formalised but make sure it is in a private atmosphere with no distractions like the television or your phone. Listen to what other members of the family are saying and respect their feelings and opinions even though they may, and will differ. Try to avoid getting on the defensive and this will generally be avoided if you really listen to what the other person is saying and the feelings they are expressing.

Repeat back what the other person says if you are having trouble understanding and try to show by your body language that you now do so. Do not minimize their feelings by saying they are being dramatic or wrong for feeling how they feel. Speak the way that you would want someone to speak to you.

Family members often disagree about how they should deal with their personal problems. While it may be difficult to hear, sometimes it's good to have a family member share another perspective of a situation. This enables the person dealing with the issue to make an informed decision about what troubled them.

Communicating with a Service Provider

In many ways this can be one of the most challenging areas of communication but in many ways one of vital importance. This is because our specific mission is to get something done, resolved or clarified. Irrespective of whether the service provider is a bank clerk, a telephone responder, a home handyman their job is to help you. Unfortunately, in this current and complex tele- communications age by the time we reach them the situation is often causing us a degree of frustration which can seriously impact on our mission which is to get something done or resolved.

Very often the situation is complicated by inadequate staffing and by our assuming that our correspondent has more authority than they have and can change the rules at random. So, the question is: *Will my frustration and the actions it leads to solve my problem?*

Telephone service providers, perhaps more than anyone, suffer the indignity of anger much of the time. Often when when the customer has waited with ever increasing impatience to a message that advises that their call is important. What a change it must make to their day and the success of your call if they hear. *"How are you doing? You guys must be busy to day I've waited quite a while"* instead of an opening blast *"at long last, your company must be one of the worst service providers in Canada".* There is an expression that *"you get more flies with honey than vinegar."* How true.

CHAPTER 6
Effective Public Speaking

Introduction to public speaking... Basic guide lines Preparation and Practice...Establishing confidence and note referral...Creating your winning speech ... Mission (AIM) ... Structure ... Hook ... Content ... Close... Your body language...Sound...Use of words...ideas.

Many people will at one or another time in their life be asked to make a speech, a request that can take many forms. A wedding speech by several different members of the wedding party, an after-dinner speech at a banquet, a business information talk, a motivational speech at a sales meeting, or even a eulogy at a funeral. The list is in fact almost endless.

For those who pursue public speaking as a hobby or profession, the thrill of speaking in public is an exhilarating challenge but to many others it is an almost fearsome prospect. However, for both, there are many challenges and skills that have to be faced and developed. Fortunately, these skills can be learned in order to make the presentation meaningful and memorable. This is a challenge that all speakers must face.

For some, the ability to make a confident and interesting speech comes naturally but for most people it has to be learned in order to be mastered, and then like most skills we master, public speaking becomes enjoyable.

In this chapter we are going to take a step-by-step approach to the creation of an award-winning speech from idea to construction to presentation. The first things to consider are some basic guide lines.

Basic Speech Guidelines

- Understand who you are.

We are best at speaking about what we are interested in and know something about. Personal interest, especially a passionate interest, invariably creates enthusiasm. That is quickly picked up by an audience which in turn inspires us to greater performance.

- Circumstances of the speech.

We perform better when we are fully aware of the territory and circumstances of the speech. What are the audience's expectations? What is their knowledge of the subject under discussion? Are they there voluntarily or under an obligation? Are they likely to be pre-disposed to your subject or will it need a greater degree of persuasion?

Without being elitist, it is important to assess, if possible, the educational, linguistic and professional level of an audience. A lecture on IT research in the 21st century will obviously suggest a higher level of competence and understanding for a group of IT professionals than for a group of senior citizens, and a lecture on life in Canada for a group of new Canadians would often suggest a simpler linguistic level.

Also to be considered, are availability and suitability of equipment, who is to set it up, time frames of the presentation, how definite must be the closing time and details of preceding or subsequent speakers if any.

All of these above factor's effect both the quality, of your speech and the confidence with which you deliver it.

- Sources for research.

It goes without saying that it is imperative that you know what you are speaking about and have the credibility and depth that knowledge brings.

It may certainly take a lifetime's work and research to become an expert in a general field. It is however far less demanding to become an expert in a specific and more limited field. Make that field your niche, develop a passion for it and pursue the numerous facilities available to widen your knowledge.

You will almost always find individuals in an audience wo are better informed than you are and who sometimes will try to make that obvious by asking difficult questions. However, if for instance you are discussing agriculture and do not know the best seeding time for Carrots the audience will forgive you far more easily than if you put yourself out as an expert on carrot husbandry.

Part of your research responsibilities are to be aware of the facts in your specific field and to be able to defend them along those areas which are controversial. We will be looking later at the most advantageous ways of answering questions.

- Speech structure.

Your speech must be structured in such a way that your audience can quickly understand the premise (hook), can easily follow its analysis (content) and finally fuse the hook and content together (close).

The *"a priori"* condition of all speeches is of course that the speaker's message be understood. Later in this chapter we will discuss speech construction in much greater detail.

- Practice.

It is said that practice makes perfect. This may not be totally true as perfection is a skill few of us attain. However, there is no question that it vastly improves your speaking style. Churchill, perhaps one of our greatest contemporary orators, one said that a good 10-minute speech requires at least 10 hours of practice and another 10 in preparation.

Practicing your body language, sound, and emphasis in front of a mirror or an objective and supportive friend and perhaps with audio visual equipment will turn your speech into a masterpiece. It will at the same time increase your self-confidence.

There is a circle of development here which can be clearly observed. Practice enhances confidence, confidence improves delivery and improved delivery encourages greater perfection (practice).

Finally, it is regular practice that emphasises that the words you have chosen are the correct ones and if not gives you the opportunity to change them.

- Establishing confidence and note referral.

Having said that regular practice creates confidence there are also several other negative factors which can also have an impact. These have to be considered quite early before giving a speech and which if ignored will likely impact negatively upon it. These are: lack of preparation, lack of prior knowledge, inappropriate expectation, audience fear and audience questions. Let us look at each of these.

- Lack of Preparation and prior knowledge.

Know what you are talking about. Establish and remember the facts to support your opinion or position. Your degree of preparation depends to a great extent on what your audience expects both of the speech and your knowledge. If you do not know or are not as sure of your subject as you should be, make sure that you differ between opinion and factual statement. An audience is far less critical of a reasonably based opinion with which they might disagree, than a fact they know is wrong. Make no mistake, if it is wrong someone will tell you about it.

Think carefully about what you are trying to achieve and the degree to which your words and structure will achieve that objective. Remember a speech is not for your benefit, but for the benefit of your audience.

- Inappropriate expectation.

An important part of preparation is being fully aware of the mission of the speech and the audience's expectations. Many speeches are pre-promoted by publicists at all levels as being able to do x, y or z but do not check with the speaker as to what they are actually able to deliver. For example: Are they expecting a deeply informative speech on a subject of specific interest? Ask yourself how relevant and important is that interest, what precisely do they want to know, how well can they absorb it? Do they on the other hand want to be entertained, inspired, guided? What do you think is the best way to do this? If you do not do this, do not know their expectations and do not then fulfil them they will be irritated at their loss of time and even annoyed.

- Audience fear.

Many novice speakers tend to regard the audience as the *"enemy"* who are basically there to criticise. When a speaker has delivered enough speeches however, they realise very quickly that this is not the case and the average audience is benevolent.

Almost without exception, most audiences want to be entertained in the broadest sense of the word and are almost universally forgiving. There are sometimes one or two individuals who do not fit this benevolent assessment but fortunately a good speaker knows how to diplomatically disarm them knowing that the people in the audience have probably met these kinds of people many times their own lives.

- Audience Questions

Many speakers dread this part of a presentation, believing, (usually wrongly), that the questionnaire is trying to trick them. This is almost invariably not the case, but they are seeking clarification. If you have researched your subject sufficiently you should be easily able to handle this.

However, there are some factors of which the speaker should be aware.

1. The questionnaire is not expecting a *"secret of the universe"* answer, but one that fits their immediate area of general concern.

2. They do not expect an immediate response which they will probably realise has been pre-planned. Take your time in answering and they will believe that they have received the best answer possible in the circumstances.

3. Do not be afraid to admit that (a) there is a lack of universal agreement or (b) a confusion in your mind which only merits an opinion or (c) that you do not know.

Most people do not expect the *"wisdom of the universe."* What they do expect is an honest searcher for the wisdom of the subject at hand.

The aim and style of your speech.

This is significantly different from the actual style of the speaker which we will look at later. Before a speaker begins to craft a speech the first question they should ask of themselves is what is their aim or goal? what do they hope to achieve? and what is the reason they are giving the speech?

These questions are imperative because each type of speech should be mainly directed by a separate set of skills. It is important to remember however, that although all of a speaker's skills can be included, the speech itself, should be guided by one specific goal.

Generally speaking, there are three types of speech although there are many sub-sections of each type. A helpful acronym will help you remember these divisions:

What is my AIM? where:

A = Amuse or entertain.

I = Inform or educate

M = Motivate or persuade

The Amusing or entertaining speech.

Let us look first at the amusing or entertaining speech. Examples of this could be a speaker at a wedding, an after-dinner speaker for any occasion, a keynote speaker for an occasion where a light hearted speech would be appreciated or a roast for a retiring employee. There are several main secrets to delivering an amusing or entertaining speech.

(1) Pauses. Appropriate pauses are imperative in order for the any humour to *"sink in"* and be understood as it may take some people a while longer. However, there is a subtle imperative here, as the speaker must feel, often instinctively and quite quickly, that the comment was not amusing and move on. This is a skill which comes with practice.

(2) Surprise. If an audience is expecting the punch line of a humorous remark or roast, they generally will not laugh. Therefore, the humour must generally be unexpected and if possible new and unique. Let me give two examples I recently witnessed which are fine examples of the genre.

In a speech complimenting the bride, the groom's father gave a long list of highly positive adjectives to describe her. Upon reaching the last one however, he hesitated and referring to his notes said to the bride *"I'm sorry Anne I can't read your notes"* and walked over to ask her to translate.

In a second, a keynote speaker humorously discussed his fear of small rooms. When he was a child, he explained that he used to hide in a small closet to read. Upon emerging one day he was told that while in there his patents had been eaten alive by a wild penguin *(element of surprise)*. The punch line however, was when he said he was distraught about it as he had *never seen a penguin*.

(3) A sense of the ridiculous. Mark Twain once said *"It is one type of humour to laugh at a Unicorn, an animal that could exist but doesn't, but an entirely different type of humour to laugh at a rhinoceros which looks as though it shouldn't exist but does."* At the heart of this comment is I believe the ability to alternate between a reasonable or rationale scenario and one that is not. This promotes the constant element of surprise. i.e.

"I was walking down our local hight street last Sunday morning *(reasonable)* and I bumped into a large, wild penguin *(unreasonable and therefore surprise)*. I was surprised at this *(reasonable)*, as I thought penguins went to church on Sunday *(unreasonable and therefore surprise)*. He then walked over to me *(reasonable)* and telling me that he was hungry asked for the Local McDonald's" *(unreasonable and therefore surprise)*

(4) Exaggeration.

As with telling a good story it is the speakers right (or even obligation) to exaggerate a scenario while still maintaining a believable truth.

(5) Unique scenarios.

An entertaining speaker may not necessarily be humorous as they can certainly have many different styles. However, most entertaining speakers normally search for an approach or subject which is unique or generally outside the experience of the average listener i.e., personal experiences, travel dialogues, or unusual and little-known information based on their own expertise or interest.

A good friend who for many years was a well-known journalist took early retirement and now makes a reasonable retirement income lecturing on the Jack the Ripper case. Many people know the general background, but very few know it to the well-researched extent that he does. His lectures discuss in detail the many different theories, the most plausible, his own, the social environment and character of the personalities involved.

The Informative Speech.

Let us take a look now at the specifics of an informative or educational speech and how it differs in style from a humorous one. The essence of an informative speech is that its mandate is to present information in such a way that it is understood and remembered. This is obviously far different from an entertaining speech and requires a different approach.

The most important aspects of an informative and educational speech are structure, clarity and explanation. Structure: The mission must be clear from the very beginning (the hook). *"Tonight, I am going to explain in detail, the various aspects and advantages of our new pension plan."* Those details should then be briefly described in bullet form. i.e *"I'm ging to describe the benefits of the new plan, then how it compares to our previous one and then specifically what is covered.*

An informative speech should be geared to the needs of the specific group and clarity both of words and construction is imperative.

A motivational, inspirational or persuasive speech.

An effective motivational, inspirational or persuasive speech does not require the surprise/pauses etc of an entertaining speech nor the structure of an informative one, but it does require a more powerful use of words. It is these in their proper sequence that will inspire and by-pass both logic and structure and appeal directly to the emotions which is imperative in this type of speech.

There are several main criteria for an effective motivational, inspirational or persuasive speech and one very specific one for a persuasive speech. An inspirational speaker should try to cover as many of these as possible

<u>What's in it for me.</u>

All speeches have a subjective aspect but an inspirational one even more so. The listener will be mainly concerned with the following:

- how will this particular speech help them?

- will this speech affect their way of looking at the world and in particular their place within it?

- will it have an Ah! Ah! moment when they see things differently?

- is it so thought provoking that they will leave the room pondering on its deeper significance?

- does it impact upon their own life's experiences?

- does it touch or evoke their emotions?

- will it evoke the emotions of the audience as a whole and the individual in particular?

- will it prompt them to act?

- does it evoke a sense of urgency?

- does it encourage them to believe in the practical possibility of very real change in their attitude, behaviour or conviction?

- personal belief. Do they believe in the speaker's personal conviction?

- how was that achieved?

In order to satisfy these needs effective motivational speakers should be seen to believe in what they are saying. Human instinct is often infallible in this area and a phony can often be quickly detected. Sad to say however, this is frequently not the case. It is imperative that verifiable examples of dynamic change be given and the idea promoted that this is possible, due more to a change of attitude, belief and perception than to more strenuous effort.

The final and indeed most powerful tool in the motivational speaker's skill set is their use of words. These are described in detail in the previous chapter.

Once a speaker has decided on their aim (amuse, inform or motivate) they must then proceed to the actual task of creating the speech itself.

Structure of a Speech

Usually, und with very few exceptions an effective speech should have:

A Hook: to get the attention of the audience

Content: to keep their attention AND

An Effective Close: so they will remember the speech and why they spent time listening to it.

Each of these demands a different application of ideas. Let us look first at the hook.

The Hook.

It is safe to say that the hook is the most important part of a speech and should generally take only a minute or so.

In all new social interactions, it is the first few minutes that serve to get the attention and interest of the other person or group. Your smile, posture, self-confidence, quality of speech and eye contact are all vitally important. Examples abound:

The new boss is being introduced to their staff for the first time, a job interview, that magical moment when you see someone at a party in whom you are interested and you walk over and start to talk. If you have not ignited sufficient interest in those first few moments, it can often be an uphill battle to get it from then on. It is exactly the same in a speech.

Fortunately, you do not have to be a creative genius to construct an attention getting hook because there are many and a few examples are suggested below.

Flamboyant. The speaker runs onto the stage and demands your attention *"because if you concentrate on me in the next 5 minutes instead of laying on the beach in Cuba, your life will change forever. Are you ready to have your life changed?"* Where this type of hook is concerned make sure you are fully aware of the culture of your audience. Some will enjoy and welcome it but others may resent its apparent insincerity.

Controversial. *"It is my belief that employment insurance and all forms of social assistance encourage laziness and are an abuse of tax payer's money. In the next few minutes, I will explain why."* The speaker may certainly not have the support of the audience but will certainly have their attention.

Dramatic. *"Did you know that you will collect more life destroying bacteria by putting your hand on a subway seat or handrail than washing your toilet bowl for a year. In my presentation tonight I will--"*

Emotional. *"Are you aware that while you are sitting in this comfortable, well-lit and warm room there are millions in sub-Saharan Africa dying daily of starvation?"* There is however, one important caveat about an emotional speech or hook. Believe sincerely in the sentiments you are expressing. Human instinct is almost infallible in this area and if you are not, your audience will at best ignore you or at worst despise you. Sadly, there are many popular and populist speakers who ignore this important caution.

<u>Thought Provoking</u>. *"There have been more advancements in science and technology in the last 50 years that in the previous 1000 and more in the last 20 than in the last 50. The question we must ask, as an evolving society, is this. Are we in charge of the dynamic of change or like the religions of old is it in charge of us? Ladies and Gentlemen, my subject tonight is -----"*

<u>Humorous</u>. Humour is often a great way to get attention but it must not just be the telling of a joke. The joke should relate either to the subject matter or the speaker in some way, as otherwise it will often be perceived as just a cheap way of getting attention.

Speech Content

In terms of speech construction and formatting the content is often the easiest part of a speech because the hook has generally set the tone.

The content should expand, explain and justify the major premise of the hook. If indeed it has not already been done in the hook, it is generally important to outline the subjects under discussion in bullet or point form.

The reason for this is quite simple when it is remembered that the purpose of effective content is to keep the attention of the audience rather than to initially achieve it. Your audience may not be interested in every aspect of your discussion but if you outline them, they will wait attentively, not knowing of course exactly when their point of interest is going to come.

A structured set of points serves the additional advantage of keeping the speaker on track. There is nothing more frustrating that a speaker who digresses and wanders from topic to topic.

For instance, an investment broker looking for new customers may start his content as follows. *"My friends, in my presentation tonight I am going to describe the recent 20-year history of investing in Canada, I will follow this by a brief discussion of the current state of the market, then with this as our base point show how you can make a guaranteed return on your investment of at least 12% and finally we will look at future trends"*

Listeners may not be interested in the first point. Marginally in the second, totally in the third and probably not in the fourth. However, they will not know when each will be presented and will therefore generally listen attentively to all.

An important extra aspect of your content that should not be overlooked is in relation to a speech of a persuasive nature. It is not overly beneficial to immediately present your arguments in favour of your premise. If you do this the other side will probably not listen because they are marshalling theirs.

The secret is to present the other side's arguments as honestly and objectively as possible, and having done so, defeat theirs by the superior logic of yours. This is generally known, but rarely practiced as the pre-emptive approach and can be used in almost every situation including one-on-one discussions, group discussions, negotiating, public speaking or indeed any situation where persuasion is a goal.

Let us give an example of this sort of opening approach. Suppose you are trying to persuade an audience that there should be strong legislation to prevent the ownership of firearms. Your aim is (a) to persuade them to listen to you and then (b) to begin to believe in your opinion. You might begin your speech as follows:

"Let us begin by saying that I fully understand the reluctance of many people to support this legislation. Like you, I too agree with the freedom of choice and the right to bear arms as outlined in our constitution. It is obvious that we are treading on tricky ground to even challenge these freedoms which are its bulwark. I do so with great caution and full respect for your opinion.

I fully accept the premise that people and not guns kill people, that protecting our home and civil liberty is basic to our survival and that it is tradition that ultimately holds any society together.

However, to every premise and belief there is an equivalent God given right to challenge it and my challenge is that rules, laws and, behaviour, have to reflect changing times, failing which we would never have emerged from the caves or the dark ages and it on that basis and with respect to you all, that I present my challenge."

The Close

The purpose of the close is to encourage your audience to remember the speech and why they listened to it in the first place. Hopefully you have presented a challenging premise in your hook. In the content you have proven, explained and justified your premise.

Now is the chance to fuse both together in a fully proven statement and summary of your premise. This should be an opportunity to suggest that your audience do something, feel something, do some research, write to their member of parliament, review their insurance portfolio, think about their attitudes, re-evaluate their life's direction or to practice sone of the suggestions introduced in your premise.

Drama, emphasis and indeed passion can be an important part of this, as this is your final moment to fully connect your audience with your speech.

It is not sufficient to merely repeat. This is the time where emotion and reason have to be fused together so that each reinforce each other.

Your ultimate purpose is to have your listener leave the room with the words wow!!! on their lips and a solid belief that they have heard something significant.

Summary of some general tips on improving your specific speaking skills

- Know your subject and what you want to say about it and be clear and precise when you say it.

- Study your audience (coughing/attentive/tired, how they sit).

- Use congruent body language.

- Use narrated word pictures and body language to bring the audience in and to inspire their imagination.

- Rehearse and deliver without notes.

- Vary pitch, tone and speed and make effective use of pauses.

- Surprise your audience by changes in the mood of the speech itself and your personal style i.e. Serious-humorous, intensive-casual, emotional-analytical didactic-interactive.

CHAPTER 7

Effective Public Speaking
– some more specifics

The subtle art of effective debate...Persuasion techniques... Spontaneous speaking ... Dealing with questions and answers.

The Art of Effective Debate

A debate is a formalised discussion where each of two sides of a pre-determined opinion or resolution compete. This differs from a general discussion where there is no competition, although many of the principles remain the same. The mission of a debate is for one side to persuade an audience or an appointed judge of the correctness of their opinion.

Rules of debate.

1. There are two teams, each consisting of two, three or sometimes four speakers.

2. Each team has two or three constructive/rebuttal speeches usually of 5, 3 and 2 minutes respectively. The affirmative side gives the first constructive speech, and the rebuttals alternate: negative, affirmative, negative, affirmative with the affirmative having the first and last speeches of the debate. Rebuttal speeches analyse the defects both in logic and fact of the previous speech

while introducing further factors affirming their position.

3. The affirmative must advocate only on the topic itself. No revision is permitted during the debate.

4. The onus is on the affirming side to prove their position by providing sufficient evidence to convince a reasonable audience that it is more reasonable to believe their assertion than to disbelieve it. Facts must be accurate. Visual materials are permissible, and once introduced, they become available for the opponent's use if desired.

5. Each speaker can be questioned as soon as they conclude their speech and must do so without consulting their colleagues. Questions must be fair and clear and have a direct bearing on the issue under debate. In the questioning period, the questioner may ask any fair, clear question that has a direct bearing on the debate, must confine themselves to questions and not make statements, comments, or ask rhetorical questions.

6. No new constructive arguments can be introduced in the rebuttal period. The affirmative must, if possible, reply to the major negative arguments before the last rebuttal.

Tips for a successful debate.

1. <u>Anticipate and disarm</u>. In almost any form of negotiation, and a debate is a form of negotiation, the

opposing side will have both an opinion which they will address as well as an opinion as to why you are wrong.

The opening debater proposing the affirmative, should try to anticipate those opposing arguments, present them first as part of their opening position, and then to weaken them by superior logic. The second speaker in their rebuttal should do the same by anticipating as many of the affirmative's arguments, demolishing them and presenting their own.

This method of presenting your "opponents" (for want of a better word) arguments first, works effectively not only in debate but in almost every other social situation from a business negotiation to a minor family squabble. For example: your teenager won't tidy their bedroom. Instead of *"you must keep your bedroom tidy"* so much better to say. *"Look Pete"* (assuming it's a Pete rather than a Pat) *"I know it's your bedroom and you feel comfortable as it is and it really shouldn't bother me but I'm scared that if you don't keep it cleaner a man-eating cockroach will emerge from under your bed"* etc, etc, etc. Light hearted humour can often work.

2. Presentation of provable and unprovable facts.

A good tip is to present indisputable facts followed by unprovable generalised back up, where logic is lost in the middle. i.e. Smoking causes cancer (indisputable) and billions die each year from related respiratory diseases (unprovable). In accepting the first they are usually prepared to accept the latter without detecting the difference.

3. The power of false analogy.

A false analogy is a powerful persuasive technique in which, if two things are alike in one respect, they are automatically assumed to be alike in another. The fact that two things are alike in one respect however, does not lead to the conclusion they must be alike in some other one. The astute debater should always be on the alert for a false analogy, many of which can be quite subtle. For example:

"In time rain can wear down the tallest mountain, so time can solve all our problems"

"A watch is very complex and has a designer therefore the complex universe must also have one" (i.e. God)

"I don't believe in Ghosts because I've not seen one"

"Telephones and bananas have a similar shape and fit into our hands. Telephones have a designer so must bananas"

"Many addictions destroy people's health so being addicted to reading and coffee will do the same"

Of course, if you are rebutting you have to recognize when your opponent is using these arguments and then rebut them for their *"atrocious lack of logic."*

4. Metaphor.

A metaphor is a comparison between two things that aren't basically alike. However, they will have enough in common to distract a speaker's audience to other, deeper and often more emotional issues. Usually, its main purpose is to dramatically emphasise a point.

In a debate however, its main purpose is to distract and muddy the waters of the issue at hand. Examples with the metaphor underlined and in italics:

"When I try to understand the affirmatives lack of logic *I wallow in the muddy waters of illusion*"

"Having rules in a society does not imply being locked *in a dark cage of restraint* (debate on limits of freedom)

"Having English as a Universal language does not mean living our lives in a *cultural desert*" (Debate on having English as a Universal language)

Perhaps one of the greatest speeches of our time where repeated metaphor had a profound effect was Martin Luther King's speech *"I have a dream"* which the writer sincerely believes is the greatest contemporary speech ever made. A small example with metaphor underlined follows:

"This momentous decree came as a great beacon light of hope to millions of Negro slaves who had been seared in the flames of withering injustice. It came as a joyous daybreak to end the long night of their captivity.

But one hundred years later, the Negro is still not free. One hundred years later, the life of the Negro is still sadly crippled by the manacles of segregation and the chains of discrimination"

5. Generalisation.

A generalisation applies when a factor which applies to a limited area of application is wrongly but equally applied to a wider one. When debating or speaking generalisations are often difficult to catch as they are frequently used but, in a debate, or a speech, they can make all the difference between truth and fallacy.

Examples:

"French people like cooking" does not mean that all French people like cooking.

"Most Indian spices used in cooking are good for you" does not mean that all spices are good for you.

"Russians drink a lot of Vodka" does not mean that all Russians do.

6. The Slippery slope.

The slippery slope argument is generally one of the oldest and most frequently used tools in both debate, speaking and often political discussion. This suggests that if a premise is presumed to factually exist every possible progression or evolution of it is equally feasible and even just as factual. Examples abound:

- Being permitted to withdraw medical treatment for a terminal and in pain patient will lead to euthanizing Grandma who is costing too much to support in a nursing home.

- Banning cigarette smoking in bars will lead to a police state where anything of which the government does not approve is a criminal offence.

- Imposing tariffs on imported good to help a local economy will lead to economic isolationism.

- Banning guns will lead to banning all forms of civil protection including door-locks and the police.

- A watch is very complex and has a designer therefore the complex universe must also have one.

The defects in logic in all of the above are blatantly obvious but in the heat of debate or the stress of evaluating a speech they can be easily overlooked.

Spontaneous Speaking.

There are many times you may be asked to give an opinion or to give a short speech at a moment's notice generally allowing you no time to prepare. This could well be at a business meeting, maybe in the street by a passing news hound, in a public social gathering, at a community meeting or at a wedding.

Spontaneous speaking or Table Topics at a Toastmaster's meeting is just that, practice at giving an informed opinion without preparation. To some it is the most difficult part of an evening but to others, it is often the most entertaining. In either case here are some guidelines which can make it easier.

1. <u>Take your time</u>. Do not think that you have to respond immediately. You will have much greater credibility, audience interest and success if you think for a few moments about what you going to say.

2. <u>Focus on the topic</u>. The question you are asked, or the topic you are given, may have several secondary factors but only one focus. Identify the focus as soon as you can and dismiss the rest.

3. <u>Summarise your opinion</u>. Quickly summarise your opinion or reply in your mind in a few words, six or seven at most. Then having done so, an expansion of them is quite easy.

The question for example *"Would you prefer to be rich or intelligent"* does not require an analysis of all the reasons but merely. *"I want to be intelligent"* The padding will follow.

4. <u>Open with a solid factual sentence.</u>

5. <u>Close by repeating your opening sentence.</u>

<u>Questions and Answers</u>

There will be times at the end of a speech that the speaker may be asked questions.

These are two main reasons for this (a) to clarify issues that are not clear or (b) to test the speaker's credibility. In many ways these can be the most important part of a presentation in that they not only clarify and define the audience's understanding of the subject, but confirm, or in some cases negate the credibility of the speaker.

However, questions should be avoided if the speaker believes that their audience is basically hostile, are in fundamental disagreement or if the speaker is not secure in their knowledge. Assuming however, that this is not the case and the speaker has decided on a question-and-answer session here are some tips that will prove invaluable.

Listen carefully

The listeners question may be mixed with other less obvious issues which may act as red herrings. What exactly are they asking and why? Is there a deeper issue that may not be immediately apparent? What is their personal involvement and concern? is there an emotional issue that will not be answered by logic?

Repeat

Repeat the question clearly and slowly and indicate that you are thinking of your reply so that both the speaker and the audience understand the issues. This will of course give you a little extra time to formulate your response.

Simplify

Repeat the question in the most simplistic way possible. A complicated question which may confuse the audience can be easily restated in a simplistic way that may give you a speaker's advantage.

Example: *"Given the present state of the economy and the vast amount spent on dealing with the present economic crisis. What effect will it have on future economic predictions.* Answer. Rebound the question. *"What's going to happen economically?"*

Opinion or fact?

When you present a fact make sure it is factual and backed by sufficient resource material. If in any doubt cover this uncertainty by:

"I understand that ----- "
"It would seem that ---"
"It is generally accepted that -----"
"In my opinion -----"

If in doubt generalise and obfuscate.

"There are too many unemployed in this country"

"It is generally believed that -----"

Irrelevant questions

Some people do like the sound of their own voice to the degree that they will be tempted to ask a question that is not relevant to the subject under discussion. If this is obvious to you, as often it will be, it will also be obvious to the audience and it will then become an opportunity to be assertive without offending the wider group. *"Thank you for your question but I don't think that it is relevant to the subject under discussion."*

<u>Divert the issue but do not fake an answer</u>

Sometimes a person may ask a question just for the purpose of participating rather than as a sincere enquiry. If you do not know a specific and effective answer it is always reasonable to divert the question into more familiar lines.

Politicians who are often the front-line in media questions are usually masters at this. They know that the interviewer is obliged to ask questions and that the interviewee is obliged to answer, irrespective often of relevance. A typical diversionary answer to the following could be:

Question: *"but don't you think that evidence shows that our food contains many carcinogens"*

could be

Answer: *"Most industries are very safety conscious and constantly refine their production processes to take health, safety and security into account"*

In a technology lecture the question may be asked:

Question: *"do you not think that most modern technological products are over engineered and too complex for the public?"*

could be answered as:

Answer: *"In a modern economy all modern processes including technology have to be described and great efforts are made to simplify that process."*

Basically, the answer will satisfy the questionnaire but will probably not answer the question because this was probably not the questioner's intention.

<u>Do not get angry.</u>

It goes without saying that a speaker should not show their anger as this almost immediately loses them their credibility. Anger or irritability will almost always default the talk or lecture to one of confrontation and argument.

Not showing irritation may sometimes be difficult but it is imperative that a speaker demonstrates confidence and knowledge. People who are confident and knowledgeable are generally secure enough to face a difficult audience or member of it.

Generally simple communicative strategies can diffuse a conflicting situation or reduce it to one of intense discussion and finally to debate. When answering a hostile audience or member of it try where possible to avoid the words: *but, however* or *should (as it applies to the questioner)*, even though that may be difficult to do, as these will often negate the positivity of your response. i.e.:

"believe me, I fully understand your opinion. There are of course two sides to the issue which I have also considered."

Rather than

"but I am not sure you fully understand the situation, let me explain"

"Yes, I realise I should know the answer. I have researched it a lot and am still not confident that a real answer is out there"

rather than

"I'm sorry, but I can't know everything"

A campaigning politician might be asked:

"Why should I vote for you, you never responded to my enquiries?"

could respond

"I'm really sorry my office didn't respond. We get many enquiries and sadly some fall through the cracks. After the meeting I will stay behind and we can discuss"

rather than:

"I'm really sorry but we have lots of enquiries. Perhaps you should have followed it up with a reminder"

CHAPTER 8
Effective Speech Evaluation

> *Introduction to speech evaluation and what we should evaluate...Speech evaluation tips...five approaches to effective evaluation... Tips for the evaluated speaker.*

In that great international organisation known as "Toastmasters International" new members join in order to learn specifically how to give an effective speech and more generally how to communicate more effectively.

However, having gained confidence they realise quite quickly that there are many other skills that can be developed, including creativity and leadership. One of these many skills is speech evaluation because not only does speech evaluation encourage the development of the speaker but at the same time the experience of the evaluator.

Competent speech evaluation is one of the core experiences of Toastmasters. The evaluator has to generally evaluate a speech in a couple of minutes and in that short time has to ask: *What should I look for? What approach should I take? and how do I encourage confidence while trying to be honest and encouraging at the same time?* In this chapter I will try to cover these questions.

An important part of the Toastmasters program are the regular evaluations. Comments are sometimes made that they are often too *"flowery"* and effusive and lack appropriate criticism. These comments are sometimes valid however, it is important to understand that there are two general factors that affect our public speaking confidence. Self-confidence and basic ability. On their own neither will produce an effective speaker. If, as the writer believes communicative ability like walking, is a natural human instinct, it follows that *self-confidence will allow that natural ability to emerge and it is that which should be initially encouraged.*

Speaking ability, in other words has much more to do with confidence than competence.

Evaluations should be based, not on how far a speaker should reach but by *how far they have come.* An effective evaluator recognises this and evaluates accordingly. By this criterion a nervous but enthusiastic "new" speaker may well make a mediocre speech and be *correctly* evaluated as excellent, compared to an experienced but complacent DTM (Distinguished Toastmaster) with a "better" speech who is *correctly* evaluated more negatively.

An effective evaluation should be "tougher" on an experienced speaker and they should accept this as part of their development. However, *honesty, sensitivity and courtesy should always prevail.*

General Evaluation Tips.

Evaluate – not perform.

This is not about you the evaluator. *Your* speaking opportunities are on another occasion. This is about you serving the speaker by listening, observing and giving a balanced critique.

Consider the speaker's objectives,
level and sensitivity.

This involves knowing something of the speaker's background, interests and competency level.

Personalise your language.

There is a big difference between offering words of encouragement and handing down a sentence as a judge. Your main mission should be to encourage and build self-confidence not to discourage it.

An evaluator should generally be an experienced speaker to enable them to do both.

"Could you have ----?"
instead of
"You should have"

*"I think that you could have made
your hook a little stronger by -----"*
instead of
"You didn't have a very effective opening hook."

*"I believe that your premise could be
made a bit stronger by ----"*
instead of
"Your basic premise was quite vague"

Promote self-esteem.

Our self-esteem is created by the positive feedback we receive from others. Even with a really novice speaker there will be some positive aspect that the evaluator should search for. It can range from something quite minor as in complimenting them on actually getting up to speak *(perhaps for the first time)*, their courage in speaking in a second language before an audience, uniqueness of subject choice, interesting background *(important in an ice-breaker)*, an interesting opinion or subject.

Even something like a compliment on a speaker's engaging smile or confident manner. It does not take too much observation to find these *"sparks of gold,"* but to a speaker they are priceless.

Avoid whitewash.

Subject to the comments made in the introduction, remember that an evaluation serves no purpose if it contains nothing more than just flattery, empty platitudes and compliments. Its purpose is to offer an honest and objective critique, both passively and where appropriate, negatively. The secret however, is to be able to use the power of words to offer it in a constructive manner.

An excellent technique is what is referred to as the sandwich method where a "do better" critique is sandwiched between positive comments both at the beginning and end.

Decide in advance what you are going to evaluate
(see - approaches to evaluation - in the next section).

A full and comprehensive speech could well take 30 minutes or more, however, most opportunities to do so are only for a few minutes at best. It is therefore imperative that the evaluator decide what they are going to watch for. If they do not do this their evaluation will usually be littered with useless phrases such as:

"That was a great hook" (why and how?).

"I loved your close" (what was great about it?)

"Your word descriptions could have been stronger." (? example)

"It was an interesting subject" (what made it interesting?)

"That was the best speech you have ever made." (what made it such a masterpiece so that I can do it again?)

Focussing, as we will see is vital to an effective and constructive evaluation.

Be subjective.

Let it be clear that your evaluation is not based on some universal criteria of excellence but only on the evaluator's subjective viewpoint. This can and should be based on the evaluator's own personal experience and knowledge but ultimately what impresses and interests them can and will always be subjective.

It is important for a speaker, especially a novice to realise this, especially when they feel that a *"do better"* may not be fair or warranted.

FIVE APPROACHES TO EVALUATION

As mentioned above you generally only have time to evaluate a few aspects of a speech. You should therefore determine your approach in advance and only evaluate that area. Unless, of course, something particularly noticeable comes up. The following are five approaches that are recommended.

Approach to Structure.

In this approach you evaluate the overall structure of the speech and not the speaker's style or performance. An approach to structure can be broken down into three areas. Hook, body and close.

Hook. Did the speaker "grab" your attention? How did they do so? Could they have done better and if so how? What other methods would you suggest?

Body. Did the speaker retain your attention? How did they do so? Could they have done it better and if so how? Did you understand the message, direction and points that were made? Did the content of the body relate sufficiently to the opening premise? Was it structured in such a way as to provide the listener with a sense of direction?

Close. Did the speaker justify your listening to the speech? was there a *"call to action?"* If not how could they have done so? will you remember the speech? If so, why and if not, how could they have made you do so? Did the close adequately summarise and *"prove"* the mission or premise of the speech as outlined in the hook? How did they do so? if not, can you give an example of how they could have done so?

Approach to Style.

In an approach to style, you evaluate the speaker's style of delivery and *not* content. Style can be broken down into three areas. Sound, body language and personality factors.

Sound. This in itself can be discussed in at least five areas:

Pitch (volume), intonation, pauses, speed and emphasis. Let us look at each in turn.

Pitch. Could you, the evaluator, hear the speaker clearly? Maybe the evaluator should stand at the back of the room for a while. All listeners have the same need to hear the speech.

Intonation. Intonation is the "melody" that is given to a sentence or phrase. Does the voice rise and fall both in emphasis and tone to maintain interest?

Pauses. Did the speaker pause long enough for the important or humorous aspects of a speech to *"sink in"* or was the speaker so nervous to get it over that they ignored this?

Tempo (speed). Did the speaker speak to quickly that the message was lost or misunderstood or did they speak so slowly that the interest waned?

Emphasis. It is suggested that effective emphasis contributes at least 45% of meaning in the spoken word as is discussed in detail later. There are obviously parts of any speech where emphasis is imperative. Did the speaker do so? If they did not, can you give them examples as to how they may have done so? There is all the difference in the world between *"I urge you to consider this"* compared with *"I urge YOU to consider this."*

Phonetic. This is the way the speaker makes each sound. Where appropriate, did the speaker clearly enunciate each sound within each word? Did their words slur into each other or was each word a separate entity? There is a great difference between:

"Mr Chairman Ladies and Gentlemen,
thank you for coming"
and
"Ladysand Gentlemen thanyoufer coming"

If you notice, this can you give an example.

Let us now move on to the second aspect of style, namely body language.

Body Language

Appropriate body language consists of congruence, eye contact, interaction, movement and posture.

Congruence. Were the speaker's words adequately and appropriately reflected in their movements?

Eye-contact. Did the speaker maintain eye-contact with everyone or just a select person or area? Did they stare or just focus in a friendly manner? There is a big difference.

Interaction. Sometimes it is appropriate to engage the audience by questions. Did the speaker do so? If not, can you give an example of the questions that could have been asked?

When they referred to someone in the audience, did they just look at them pointedly (vague) or indicate with their hand? (much more specific).

If they did this, did they point with a finger (generally rude) or indicate with an open hand? which is much more courteous and friendly.

Movement and posture. Movement is very important but only to a degree. Were their movements appropriate to the audience and speech content?

For instance, an inspirational speech usually needs more energy and movement than a purely informative one, where excess movement can distract from content.

Did they move too often and too quickly? Where did they move to and how far? A speaker who forces their audience to frequently move their heads, perhaps to avoid their view being blocked by the person sitting in front, can be annoying. What about posture? A straight back and squared shoulders always indicate self – confidence. However, there are times when it can be important to lean forward and lower the voice in order to gain the audience's complicity or to have them think upon an important point.

The words *"I want you to seriously try to understand and think about these vital issues"* would be far more effective if the speaker leaned forward slightly in a mildly conspiratorial way lowering their voice when they did so. Finally, we come to the third area of style and one that is the hardest to qualify and that is personality.

Personality Factors. This includes basic enthusiasm, intensity, passion, charisma, sincerity, a basic non-intimidating friendliness, certainly a genuine smile and of course just plain old "sizzle"

An excellent way for an evaluator to make this very subjective judgment is to ask what it is that truly endears them to someone they love or admire. These will of course differ person to person, and then see if the speaker has some of those qualities, or without too much effort could adopt them.

President Barrack Obama the president of the USA from 2009 – 2017 has been regarded as one of America's most charismatic leaders and has been compared to Ronal Reagan, a leader with vastly different political viewpoints. However, the similarities in style were obvious. A folksy sense of humour, obvious sincerity and a genuine interest in people.

The writer on the other hand strongly admires Sir Winston Churchill, the British war time leader for different, but equally valid reasons. Flamboyance of character both in words and manner, abundant self – confidence and the ability to command attention.

Approach to Mission

In an approach to mission, you evaluate according to (a) the specifics requested by the speaker or (b) the goals outlined in the program.

All speeches have a purpose. What was the purpose and was it clearly identified and identifiable? Was that goal achieved and if so, how?

Specific missions or goals of a speech could be for example to persuade, to entertain, to educate, to inspire, to clarify, to analyse, or to motivate. Each of these demands a somewhat different style of speaking. Was their "style" appropriate to the goal?

For example, an inspiring speech requires a stronger use of emotional and feeling words, an informative speech should have a greater emphasis on structure and approach to a speech to clarify requires the ability to describe possibly complex issues in more simpler terms.

Approach to Interest

The fourth approach that is suggested relates to the interest of the speech. This approach is both subjective and objective in that it covers the evaluator's personal and subjective interest in the speech content and objectively their opinion of the group's needs. From both perspectives however similar questions can apply.

Did the evaluator find it interesting and why? if not, how could it have been made more interesting? Every speech can be spiced up depending upon the style of the speaker. Was it appropriate to the group and its needs as perceived by the evaluator? A lecture on quantum physics may well drive an audience of engineers into raptures whereas an audience of financial investors would certainly be less so.

Other questions the evaluator should consider are whether the content was of general and public interest. Was it well researched and backed up by source references? Did the main content sufficiently expand the "hook?" Were there any noticeable "ah – ah? Moments?" Was it original in concept or a mere rehash of existing ideas? All these are relevant to an evaluation based on interest and content. Try the following short exercise.

If the speech is about a dull subject, it is suggested that at exercise similar to the above might improve interest because almost any subject can be made interesting.

Exercise

Intentionally select a potentially uninteresting subject such as potato growing, water filtration or a history of Canadian coinage or any subject that does not inspire immediate interest.

However, a few quick few minutes of research will DEFINITELY reveal some interesting factors that could be presented in a speech.

> *These coupled perhaps with manufactured enthusiasm, a touch of flamboyance and a sense of humour could well make it a potential masterpiece.*

Approach to Word Use.

Using a word usage approach is perhaps the most difficult for the evaluator but in many ways the most rewarding for the speaker in that it demands not only intense listening but wider linguistic skills than the others.

Words are to a speaker what colour is to an artist and bricks are to a builder and it is the power of words that can form the basis of real inspirational eloquence.

The questions an evaluator might like to consider in listening to a speech could be: *"Were the speaker's words too complex for the audience?* If so, make sure you give examples. *"How did each of the words support each other and did they reinforce the concept of the speech and its underlying mission?"* if so, how was this done? and if not *"how could it have been done?" "Did the speaker's words, inspire motivate or impact in some specific way?"*

When offering a compliment try to be as specific as possible and if offering a *"do better"* and based on your own experience, try to give an example. Both will show the speaker that you have really been listening. *"You used really good words"* or *"your words could have been more dynamic"* will just not be sufficient.

The English language is one of the world's finest in terms of its volume, scope and expressive capacity and there are several powerful tools that a speaker can use to turn an ordinary speech into a masterpiece.

These include: *Onomatopoeia, Alliteration, Hyperbole, Metaphor, Anaphora and Comparison.* Let us look at each of these and give some examples.

Onomatopoeia - Sound of action matches word sound. i.e., *"The Sword swished silently"* – *"He bullied his way into the meeting"*

Alliteration - Same sound at beginning of at least three consecutive words. i.e. *"She looked at him with cold calculating contempt"* – *"He rose out of bed with self-righteous revenge in his heart"*

Hyperbole - Exaggerated non-literal statements to emphasis a point i.e. *"I've told you a thousand times please put your plates in the sink"* - *"I am so hungry I could eat a horse"*

Metaphor - This is an exaggerated scenario for dramatic comparison i.e.:*" He fought like a lion"*

Anaphora - Identical repetition of the opening phrases of several related sentences (normally three or even more times). *"I have a dream"* (Martin Luther King) – *"We will fight them on the beaches"* (Winston Churchill, Britain's war-time leader) - *Barrack Obama" We can - - -* "at his nomination speech for the US Presidency.

Comparison - Dramatic comparison between realties i.e. then and now, black and white, freedom and tyranny.

Of these there is no doubt that a combination of metaphor and anaphora is the most powerful tool in the speaker's handbook.

One of the greatest (if not the greatest) speeches in contemporary history is Martin Luther King's *"I have a dream speech"* in which, by the power of anaphora and metaphor, he challenged, evoked and changed the conscience of a nation. It is strongly recommended that you listen to this entire speech on You-Tube.

In this short excerpt the use of <u>anaphora has been clearly underlined</u> and **metaphor identified in bold**.

Martin Luther King's speech.

In his iconic speech at the Lincoln Memorial for the 1963 March on Washington for jobs and freedom, King urged America to *"make real the promises of democracy."* King synthesized portions of his earlier speeches to capture both the necessity and urgency for change and the potential for hope in American society.

"I am happy to join with you today in what will go down in history as the greatest demonstration for freedom in the history of our nation.

*Five score years ago, a great American, in whose symbolic shadow we stand today, signed the Emancipation Proclamation. This momentous decree came as a **great beacon light of hope** to millions of Negro slaves who had been **seared in the flames of withering injustice**.*

*It came as a **joyous daybreak** to end the **long night of their captivity**.*

*<u>But one hundred years later</u> the Negro still is not free. <u>One hundred years later,</u> the life of the Negro is still sadly crippled by **the manacles of segregation** and the **chains of discrimination**. <u>One hundred years later,</u> the Negro lives on a **lonely island of poverty in the midst of a vast ocean of material prosperity**. <u>One hundred years later,</u> the Negro still languishes in the corners of American society and finds himself **an exile in his own land** and so, we've come here today to dramatize a shameful condition.*

*In a sense we've come to our nation's capital to **cash a check**. When the architects of our republic wrote the magnificent words of the Constitution and the Declaration of Independence, they were **signing a promissory note** to which every American was to fall heir. This note was a promise that all men, yes, black men as well as white men, would be guaranteed the unalienable rights of life, liberty, and the pursuit of happiness. It is obvious today that America has **defaulted on this promissory note** insofar as her citizens of colour are concerned. Instead of honouring this sacred obligation, **America has given the Negro people a bad check**, a check which has come back **marked insufficient funds**.*

*<u>But we refuse to believe</u> that the **bank of justice is bankrupt**. <u>We refuse to believe</u> that there are **insufficient funds in the great vaults of opportunity of this nation, and so we've come to cash this check**, a check that will give us upon demand the riches of freedom and the security of justice.*

*We have also come to this hallowed spot to remind America of the fierce urgency of now. This is no time to engage in the luxury of cooling off or to take the **tranquilizing drug of gradualism**. <u>Now is the time</u> to make real the promises of democracy. <u>Now is the time</u> to rise from the **dark and desolate valley** of segregation to the **sunlit path of racial justice**. <u>Now is the time</u> to lift our nation from the **quicksand of racial injustice** to the **solid rock of brotherhood**. <u>Now is the time</u> to make justice a reality for all of God's children"*

You will note that in this very small excerpt he has used metaphor at least 20 times. Some examples from above:

"Great beacon light of hope to millions seared in the flames of withering injustice"

"Joyous daybreak to end the long night of their captivity"

"Crippled by the manacles of segregation and the chains of discrimination"

"A lonely island of poverty"

The speech also used at least 3 examples of anaphora. Some examples"

"We refuse to believe -----"

"One hundred years later ---"

"Now is the time"

Tips for the Evaluated Speaker

We are all sensitive to criticism and negative comments may conflict with our own opinions. So, the evaluated speaker should remember:

1. Do not overreact to what the evaluator says, even though you may not like it or agree with it. This is _one subjective opinion_ given on _one_ speech by _one_ person who may _not_ be right. It is a guide however to how one person received your speech.

2. Separate yourself from the speech. This is nothing to do with your self-worth. If you did not like the evaluation, consider giving the speech again with a different evaluator, discussing it in private with the evaluator or asking others if they agree.

3. Remember habits are difficult to break. Be patient because the secret is practice.

CHAPTER 9
The Mysterious Art of Storytelling.

Narrative---pauses---surprise---mystery---message exaggeration.

The Art of storytelling has been around since our ancestors sat in dark caves, marvelled at the warmth of fire and listened to old men tell stories of their myths and heroes. In the last few hundred years most of the wisdom of our various cultures has come down to us by the printed word. But long before this and back to the beginnings of time it was by the spoken word as part of the great oral tradition of our various tribes, cultures, religions and nations.

Sometimes this has been in graphic form but more often in myth, symbol and mystical reference. However, each tried to convey wisdom, subtlety and often great advice on how to live a moral, ethical and fulfilling life.

It is not by accident that the last request of children before they go to bed is often *"tell me a story."* I firmly believe that young children live for a great part in their own imagination and this is their way of asking us to share their own private world. It is a request that we should not ignore. However, we have all listened to the inveterate teller of tales who does not really know how to do so.

I firmly believe that the secret of storytelling is that the story should contain, if possible, a sense of mystery or magic and should, more than any other speaking medium, be enlivened with narrative. If it is personal, it should be primarily based on truth but as with myth it can be enlivened by imagination and finally and if possible, should contain an ethical message.

At the end of this chapter, I have presented one of my stories from *"The Brotherhood of Ulan and Other Mysteries"* along with a personal travel experience, *"The Ghost of Omar"* that show how each of these can be presented.

So, the question is, is there a method whereby a story can be told effectively and so well that it holds the attention and interest of the listener. The writer firmly believes that there is and would like to suggest the following five tips in order to help you do so.

In my stories I have endeavoured to do all five.

Narrative

More than in any other form of speaking narrative is vitally important. Unlike an informative, humorous or an inspirational speech which require structure, surprise and effective word use respectively, a good story needs vivid description and word pictures so that the listener may actually enter the story and see and feel what you, the speaker, is trying to describe. It is generally quite easy to describe a scene with an emphasis on the actions but to use the correct adjectives, adverbs and metaphors takes a little more imagination. A simple example, will hopefully suffice.

"Last summer I was travelling in Europe and one sunny afternoon happened to find myself in this really nice little village of Sur – en – Loise. I stopped at a cosy little bistro, had a glass of wine, enjoyed the afternoon sun, revelled in the ambience of the village and felt happier than I had been for months"

The question here is, can the listener see and perhaps even taste the wine? Does the listener really know what the bistro looks like? or in fact can they imagine the village itself? However, with the addition of maybe another 20 words in can be changed into a vivid story which will catch the listener's attention.

"Last fall, when the leaves were beginning to change, I was travelling in Europe and found myself in this beautiful French village half as old as time. Cobbled streets with old gabled houses that almost touched at the top, letting the sunlight through in soft, dappled shades of light. My glass of rich red local wine and some crusty garlic bread tasted heavenly as I took in the bunches of garlic and ham hocks hanging from the ceiling. I felt happier than I had been for months"

Pauses

Having given the listener, the opportunity to imagine the scene presented by your words, it is important for you to pause long enough for them to do so.

You have to give the listener the chance to join you in your imagination. Many speakers are so anxious to get on with the story they forget the vital importance of pacing.

Voice

Variations of voice are also of vital importance in keeping the listener's attention to the narrative you have created.

Volume. (Lowering the voice, sometimes to a whisper to emphasise drama, mystery or surprise).

Intonation. (Melody, pitch and cadence) add quality and variation.

Emphasis. Adds strength to your words especially to adjectives

"A __rich red__ burgundy" said slowly and thoughtfully rather than just *"a rich red burgundy."* Generally, words give about 55% of meaning and appropriate emphasis the rest.

Mood.

The sound of the voice should be able to express changing moods and emotions. Intrigue, surprise, awe, contemplation and mystery are all different moods that can be expressed as appropriate to the story.

Mystery

As a guide to the use of mystery, watch how movie directors of suspense/horror movies keep listeners on the edge of their seat wondering what's going to happen next. In these examples, music usually creates the mood of the unfolding drama. In your case by slowing the speed, tempo and volume your voice can achieve the same effect by slowly emphasising approaching danger or surprise.

Moral

It is not always possible, but traditionally folk stories try to bring in a moral to the story, a life lesson or ethical guidance developed by thinkers of the past. In the story at the end of this chapter you will see a story that not only includes appropriate narrative and descriptive adjectives to bring the listener into the story but a life lesson or a significant point to ponder. A lesson which is intended to live long after the story is over.

Storyteller's Privilege

It is not easy to describe this important part of the storyteller's tool chest but it is in some ways the most important in order to maintain the essence of the storyteller's art.

That is to say that every story, especially a personal one should contain a strong and major element of believable truth or possibility and it should imbue the belief that the situation described could possibly happen.

However, it can, and should be overlaid by the speaker's personalised imagination, word power and credibility. The secret, and this is imperative, is that the listener must never be totally sure where the truth ends and the writers *special privilege* begins. The real secret of storytelling rests in maintaining this balance in the same way perhaps that magicians never reveal the secret of their magic, because of course effective story telling is indeed a form of magic.

In the following two short stories, you will see how I have brought these various factors into play. In the first, appropriate narrative is underlined, a sense of mystery maintained and a thoughtful lesson is provided at the end.

Although the story could just as easily be told without most of the narrative adjectives and adverbs, it would no longer be a story but *merely the description of a set of events*. Appropriate pauses and voice variation can obviously not be shown.

The Troll and the Maiden.

In the <u>dark and brooding</u> mountains of Western Norway, mythology tells us that there live a tribe of <u>very ugly</u> half-human, half-monsters called Trolls. Unfortunately, because they are very ugly, they have an unjustified reputation for being evil. Although they can sometimes be mischievous, they are however very <u>loving and kind</u>.

One morning a young male troll was fishing <u>quietly</u> in the <u>sunny</u> valley close to his <u>dark</u> mountain home when on the other side of the bank he saw a lovely human maiden. He was so entranced that he returned every morning to observe her. This was not from any sinister motive but out of an appreciation for her beauty, and slowly he fell <u>hopelessly</u> in love.

The young man knew that he could not court her in the usual way because he knew his ugliness would frighten her away. In his longing to know the beautiful maiden, he approached the old, holy man of the tribe,

<u>meditating in his cave</u> and explained his dilemma. The holy man advised him that for a fee, he would make a mask, which, if worn, would transform the young man into a handsome prince with whom the maiden would fall in love. This he did, and the maiden did indeed fall in love with him.

They eventually married, had a family and lived in a <u>lovely</u> cottage in the valley. Their life together was <u>serene</u> and happy because he was indeed a good man who <u>deeply loved and cared for his wife and family</u>.

However, one day his happiness became threatened when his wife said to him *"my beloved husband, I know you are wearing a mask. You need to know that I love you unconditionally so I want you to remove it."* The young man refused, <u>deathly afraid</u> that his happiness was now threatened. *"You must remove it"* his wife insisted <u>more firmly</u>, and once more he refused. Finally, she told him that if he did not remove the mask, she and their children would leave him forever. Slowly and with trembling hands and a fearful heart he removed his mask and underneath --- was a handsome Prince.

The big question in this beautiful story is this, who had changed the troll or the maiden?"

The sense of being there was maintained by vivid use of narrative (mainly adjectives and adverbs), the mystery by not knowing until the last sentence how this love story would end and the moral by the lesson that we do not see things as they are but as we are. A proverb taken from the Jewish Talmud.

The Ghost of Omar

(From "The Brotherhood of Ulan and
Other Mystery Stories" by Geoff Smith).

I had known my friend Billy for most of my life. Certainly, ever since I met him on our first day at Junior Kindergarten in Dersingham Road primary school in a run-down area of an equally run-down suburb of London.

As I said a tearful goodbye to my grandma on what was the first day of school, the first thing I looked around for was for someone who was as miserable and tearful as me. Misery loves company at any age and it is that of course that makes misery tolerable. The first person my eyes rested on was Beryl a very thin young lady, who out of necessity became my first girlfriend. I liked her a lot and quickly let her know how much I cared for her by putting dirt down the back of her dress and calling her twiggy face. I did not realise of course that this was not the most effective way to the female heart. Needless to say, my approach differed considerably over the next few years, however, she always remained my first true love, unrequited as it was.

However, I also remember Billy, not only because he also cried when his parents dumped him at the school but because of the speed of his recovery when we both energetically began to play chase about 10 minutes later. Thus, the pain and anguish of childhood is fortunately so often forgotten among the more tangible, and often greater terrors of growing up, growing old and saying goodbye.

We remained friends for almost the next twenty years. Through cubs, scouts and then army cadets, although he was much more successful in each of them than I. Our favourite game as ten-year-olds was being allowed to wander the back streets of London on cold, foggy, winter nights pretending that we were detectives following a sinister suspect in a murder case. Armed as we were with our standard issue plastic Smith and Wessons filled with explosive caps, we prowled the streets, following people and making detailed summaries of their addresses and activities.

Some of our most exciting experiences however were in the foggy November and December nights in London before the clean air act of 1953. Every November or December a thick impenetrable smog, a combination of dirt and sulphur used to descend on the city with a visibility often of less than 5 feet.

The worst of course was in November 1952 when thousands of old people died. We were not worried of course as we were not old and to us it was a great opportunity to frighten old ladies and make funny sounds as we emerged silently from the fog.

We were not monsters of course, but merely young kids let lose to do what they wanted. Which in retrospect is a pretty fair definition of a monster.

As we grew older Billy and I matured and became civilised as hopefully and inevitably one does. Billy becoming more cautious and thoughtful and myself equally thoughtful but a little more spontaneous. Thus, I was surprised, when at the ripe old age of nineteen I asked Billy if he wanted to go on a backpacking trip to Turkey and he agreed.

We both had some mutual friends who were teaching English in the university of Ankara and who agreed that we could stay with them as part of our trip.

Some six weeks later found us both settled in a tiny apartment in Tuzlucayir, a dusty, poorer suburb of Ankara but close enough to the University.

For the next few days, we explored this exciting city. The great Ankara castle, a fortification half as old as time, perched high on a hilltop overlooking the city, the red-tiled roofs of old Ankara's historic houses, the Anitkabir museum dedicated to Kemal Ataturk the father of modern Turkey and of course the city's many fine museums, restaurants and bazaars. The old markets became especially intriguing in the cool of the late afternoon when they came alive with the smells and fragrances of the middle east and the noise of its excitable vendors.

After a few days exploring this exciting city, our friends suggested that we go to a traditional Turkish bath. So, a few days later found us trotting enthusiastically up the front steps of a large somewhat Victorian looking building in one of Ankara's side streets. Having paid a few Lira for a towel we proceeded to the large rubber doors which formed the entrance to the main salon. However, upon looking through the small plexiglass window was a scene which to our naïve eyes was something from Dante's inferno.

A massive white tiled room filled with thick white steam greeted our eyes. Walking in and out of the steam like so many disembodied ghosts in a Steven King movie were hundreds of large, naked, hairy Turkish men. Round the sides were about a dozen granite beds on which lay more large, naked, hairy, Turkish men being apparently violently attacked by still more of the same.

Grunts of pain echoed through the rubber doors as though amplified by the mist, as each were being twisted and pummelled like newly-made pretzels in a demonic bakery. Later information informed me that this was not only massage but highly therapeutic and a possible cure of almost all known diseases and presumably many that were not, as they all looked remarkably healthy.

However, to us and our Western sensitivity it was too much. Billy panicked and myself less so. Rushing back to the reception we asked for our money back. Unfortunately, they would not do so, but seeing Billy's obvious distress the attendant quietly advised that they were not unaware of the sensitivity of foreigners and that they would give Billy a very special Masseuse. *"You can have Omar"* he said with a strange smile, which should have aroused our suspicion and which may, or may not, in retrospect have contained a hint of malice. *"Omar is kind. Omar is caring. We call him Omar the compassionate one. Please do not be afraid, Omar will take care of you."*

Thus, Billy's mind was set at ease as we proceeded into Dante's nightmare.

Ten minutes later found us settled on our own granite beds being covered in an oily foam that was generated from a large pre-war gasoline pump. Every now and then I glanced over at Billy to make sure he had not run away and he responded with a grin and a thumbs up sign that said happily *"I'm getting Omar."*

However, in a few moments his grin turned slowly from contentment to caution and from caution to abject terror, because into the room waddled Omar who certainly did not look very compassionate.

Omar was fat. Not just plump, nor even somewhat obese, but grotesque. Six hundred pounds of quivering Turkish flesh. Omar was ugly. Three days growth of dark beard covered a large bull like face. A face dominated by large reptilian eyes, a large bulbous nose and thick protruding lips. He did not have a neck. His head seemed to grow directly out of his massive shoulders so that when his eyes searched the room for Billy his whole body slowly rotated and not just his head. On his large bulging head was a small red Fez. He was naked except for his Fez, and a small loin cloth which must have obscured something truly hideous. This was Omar.

At the same moment three things happened in very quick sequence. Billy's eyes landed on Omar, Omar's eyes landed on Billy and with a scream of feral terror Billy leapt from his bed and ran in terror from the room. This was no ordinary escape but the escape of a wild animal escaping from an unknown demon. Wildly pushing away the other customers, slipping on the soapy floor and bellowing in fear Billy disappeared from sight.

Omar the compassionate, Omar the gentle, had now become Omar the angry. Angry at losing a customer, especially a tourist who was likely to give a big tip. Omar's tightening eyes landed on me. Slowly like a large slug honing in on its helpless prey Omar waddled relentlessly in my direction. Transfixed and almost paralysed with anxiety at the unfolding spectacle, I patiently waited. Putting his face a foot before my eyes and clamping my shoulder with a fist the size of a large hambone he lisped in a heavy Turkish accent *"Are you a friend of that one?"*

Judas did not betray his redeemer with as much passion as I betrayed my friend Billy. *"Me, a friend of that stupid man? Never"* and with that I flung his hand off my shoulder and ran out of the room, with I hoped a little more dignity than Billy. Billy was nowhere to be seen. I washed, changed and with growing concern for Billy, left the building. However, as I opened the large double front door there was Billy sitting on the front step, shaking and still covered in foam being laughed at by a score of young Turkish children.

Billy of course recovered quickly from his ordeal, and we continued to have a great vacation in this beautiful country with it warm and cultured people.

A few years later I came to Canada with my family, Billy moved north and we lost contact.

However, every five years or so, when I go on vacation in England, I hop on the train and visit Billy who is now a happily married grandfather of several beautiful grandchildren. When I do so we go to the local pub and over a few beers talk about old times and of our adventures together. However, for some strange reason our friendship was never quite the same because over on the other side of the room, lurking behind the curtains, waiting patiently to give his massage, is the Ghost of Omar.

Geoff Smith

About the author.

Geoff is one of Toronto's most popular and sought-after speakers on communication, public speaking, speech construction and storytelling.

He is the author of the *"The Art of Effective Living"* a dynamic tool for personal growth and *"The Brotherhood of Ulan and other Mystery Stories"* both of which are available on www.amazon.ca as both Kindle and soft cover editions.

Geoff is a 45-year member of Toastmasters International and a recipient of the DTM their highest award for speaking excellence.

For more information on Geoff's books or to invite him as a speaker visit: www.geoffsbooks.ca

The Brotherhood of Ulan
and other Mystery Stories.

In this appealing first collection you will learn of:

- A mysterious cult in the English countryside -

- A feisty teenagers dream of freedom -

- A lesson in living from a street bum -

- A spiritual revelation in Madrid -

- A magician's secret wisdom -

- A dear friend's farewell -

- A con-man's mentor -

- A madman's ghost –

- A spy's betrayal –

and many more

www.geoffsbooks.ca

The Art of Effective Living.

Effective Living is an art that can be learned, practiced and then brought into our daily modes of behaviour. In this remarkable book you will learn about:

- Understanding and strengthening relationships -

- Building self-confidence and eliminating fear -

- Repairing emotional damage from childhood -

- Meaningful change in self-esteem and love -

- Changing inner conflict into growth -

"The Effective Life is lived with a passionate belief that it is worthwhile. It is lived with a self-induced enthusiasm, an all-consuming appetite for living and with an all-transforming determination to savour life to the full. It tastes the sweets of existence and as it progressively achieves its own worthy ideals lives vigorously and to the limits of its physical, mental and emotional capacities."

From: The Art of Effective Living

Please visit Geoff at: www.geoffsbooks.ca